Daniela Mignani

The Medicean Villas
by Giusto Utens

ARNAUD

Photographs: Liberto Perugi
Additional plates: Foto Novi

© Copyright Arnaud Ed. s.r.l. 50144 Florence - Largo Liverani, 13
1st English edition May 1991
Reprinted April 1995
2nd English edition March 2004

Translation: *Stephanie Johnson*

PRESENTATION

What strikes one most about the 14 lunettes in which Giusto Utens portrayed the Medicean villas is their symbolic content. This was probably involuntary, but highly intriguing.

At the end of the sixteenth century, Grand Duke Ferdinand I commissioned the Flemish painter from Carrara (he was naturalized Italian) to paint the canvases which were to be principally documents defining property: that is to say, a catalogue of that considerable portion of the Medici property consisting of a series of villas, leisure facilities and reception areas, as well as farms and protected territories belonging to the crown.

In fact, each painting is presented with the aseptic objectivity of a cadastral report. In a bird's eye view perspective, the Flemish painter lists with impartial and scrupulous preciseness everything that is included in (or defined by) the boundaries of the properties: portals and fountains, windows and chimney pots, trees and crops, utility structures and reception areas, the labyrinth of Italian gardens and the network of access roads, the ceramic frieze at Poggio a Caiano and the farm-houses of Villa Salvetti, famous sculptures and farm haystacks. The uniting element is not the medium of light, nor the loving curiosity for reality, as is the case in the tradition of the great Italian landscape painters from Carpaccio to Bellotto. It is rather the need to list and define, as if the figurative act aimed only to transform itself into a true, scrupulous seal of property. So it happens that, through a symbolic transfer of amazing and rather disquieting efficacy, these canvases assume the shape and emblem of power absolute. One should try to picture the Giusto Utens lunettes lined up in the room at Artimino known as "the hall of the villas" and to imagine the awe that they must have more or less indirectly invoked. The implacable "portraits" of residences, farmland and woods belonging to the crown must have seemed the symbolic inventory of the whole Principality, coldly presented to the eye of the monarch by his painter, down to the minutest details, and this, to a certain degree, is the effect that they still have today.

Extending the metaphor, it was (still is) easy to think of the Grand Duchy

*as an enormous Medicean villa with precise boundaries and everything
scrupulously accounted for, where everything surely existed because the
Prince knew everything by name, and by naming it, he possessed it. Just
as in certain tales by Borges, an inventory is an act of creation and the
only proof of something's existence, and the inventory offers with this
knowledge the durable sum total of possession. In analizing them one
by one, Daniela Mignani tells us, with refined competence and a richness
of bibliographical and documented references, about the history of the
lunettes and their precious contribution to our knowledge regarding the
Medicean villas in their original aspect.*

*For the moment I wish to emphasize the symbolic trait which interests
me more than the actual quality of the pictorial rendering or even the
iconographical content; a trait which makes Utens' lunettes a privileged
means to appreciate the Florentine civilization in the age of Absolutism
and the Counter-Reformation.*

Antonio Paolucci

PREFACE

The fourteen lunettes with the grand ducal villas were painted by the mysterious Giusto Utens (a Fleming who lived at Carrara) for the villa of Artimino, that grandiose building by Buontalenti which crowned (also in the symbolic sense) the centre of the Grand Duchy's hunting reserve on Montalbano. Their symbolic significance is obvious; right from the beginning with Trebbio and Cafaggiolo in the Mugello Valley the lunettes have seemed to summarize the presence of the Medici family and their court within the region. The style used - that of a perspective without light, completely different to any previous example of luminosity as intended by Piero dello Francesco or Caravaggio with his naturalism - is something different (within the bounds of mannerism) to paintings of full artistic dignity of the type that Ferdinand I looked for in Cigoli and Passignano and more rarely in Santi di Tito, the elderly Allori or Jacopo Ligozzi.

It is the choice itself of the view-points which makes many of these perspectives strangely falsified. With the exception of a few lunettes treated as if they were customary Flemish villages high up on the horizon, (the same ones which Giulio Mancini noted as having a character more similar to "majestic landscapes" than to "village perspectives"), these unreal view-points reveal a kind of imitation that lies half-way between painting and cartography: bird's eye views reconstructed in a studio.

The pictorial rivisitation of views, which culminated in the work of Canaletto and Bellotto, followed very different paths, as Roberto Longhi reminds us: it wandered from the perspectives of Viviano Codazzi and the intensely meteorological views of Carlevaris, presupposed Baroque illusionism, but before that it passed through the awareness of naturalism by Caravaggio which was as far from Utens' world as one can imagine. The right outlook to approach the non-views of the Flemish painter is therefore one of various levels and styles of imitation of a world where Mannerism and the iconographical demands of the Counter Reformation created that barrier between what meets the eye and paintings of full artistic dignity that led to the drama of the breakaway by Caraveggio. Contemplated with Ligozzi's zoological and botanical drawings in Grand Duke Francesco's time, Utens' lunettes prove an interesting chapter in the relationship between artistic and documentary representations, a relationship that has so far seen only a first attempt at investigation with regard to the botanical gardens at an exhibition in Pisa, the home territory of Galileo.

The need was felt for a review of perspective construction methods, of the documentary aspects and of the abnormalities in scale that the perspective suffers in the portrayal of real places, and here is the review edited by Daniela Mignani to lead us gently into this inevitable preliminary discussion.

Alessandro Conti

FOREWORD TO THE RE-EDITION

The study on the lunettes painted by Giusto Utens, once more in the press, was initiated in 1980 on the occasion of the Medici exhibitions held in Florence entitled "Medicean Florence and Tuscany in Sixteenth-Century Europe" and promoted by the Council of Europe. The large Florentine event managed to involve all cultural forces in the city. The transient, spectacular apparatus characteristic of large exhibitions was backed up by a series of cultural events delving further into the various aspects of sixteenth-century Tuscan history: from the figurative arts to the collector's zeal, from territorial architecture and design, as far as science, magic and alchemy.

Together with the success decreed by the public, one of the most important results of the exhibitions was to have brought into the limelight themes which had remained at a less prominent level in artistic historiography; in particular the topic of garden and villa architecture.

Immediately after the Medicean exhibitions, congresses and studies were set up in Tuscany which opened the way for debate on the conservation of the historical Italian garden, the landscape and the architecture of the villas. The first congress of studies on the Italian Garden was held in 1981 at San Quirico d'Orcia; in May 1981 Florence hosted the International Colloquium on the Protection and Restoration of Historical Gardens, organised by the International Committee of Historical Gardens ICOMOS-IFLA; in September of the same year, a round table was conducted at the Florentine Academy of Arts and Design, during which a "Charter of Historical Gardens" was approved, a fundamental document for the protection and restoration of gardens; in 1985 a newly set-up congress at Palazzo Pitti investigated the topic of promoting knowledge and conservation of artificial grottos; in March 1989, the international congress entitled "Boboli 90" which took place in various cultural venues throughout the city tackled the methodologies for restoring historical gardens; and, finally, in September 1998, the European Heritage Day was dedicated to Historical Gardens, and in the orbit of this event, held in Florence and in Lucca, an international conference on historical gardens and parks was convened.

The theme of the villa was thoroughly researched in parallel to the history of the garden. In particular, the exhibitions dedicated to the celebrations held in 1992 in the centenary year of the death of Lorenzo dé Medici provided the occasion to study the Medicean villas more thoroughly. Finally, the great show in 1998 dedicated to "Still Life in Palaces and Villas", organised at Palazzo Pitti and in the Poggio a Caiano villa by the Florentine museums, laid the foundations for reconstituting the artistic heritage of the Medicean villas.

Every Medici villa and garden has had its own specific study since 1980, archival sources carefully being sifted through so as to piece together in detail the construction phases and distinctive features, the transfers of title and modifications over time.

The first nucleus of Medici villas under State ownership, consisting of Petraia, the gardens at Castello, Poggio a Caiano and Cerreto Guidi, became part of the Florentine museum system in 2002. This manoeuvre to join the Florentine museum circuit, fervently sought by Superintendent Antonio Paolucci, is yet another step in carrying through the project of reconstitution of the historical heritage of the Medici collections in the villas.

More than twenty years after the first edition in 1980, the cultural and bibliographical panorama surrounding the villas and their gardens has grown so much that describing it would mean substantially modifying the lay-out of this little volume.

I have, therefore, considered it more appropriate to maintain the book in its original form, devised together with Alessandro Conti, Liberto Perugi and Guglielmo Galli, whom I always remember with much affection and appreciation.

Consequently, I have limited the changes to the 1980 text and to the 1988 edition additions - the contribution of an introductory essay by Antonio Paolucci and the documentary appendix testifying to the fortune that Utens obtained through his copies. I have merely inserted into the general biography the congresses and main texts that have given great impulse to the history of the architecture of Tuscan villas and gardens. I like to remind people that in all the most important studies, Utens' lunettes are always cited as the first, authentic base of documentary reference. The essays concerning both the villas and the gardens and comparing archival documents with Giusto Utens' painted images have all confirmed the worth of faithful representation of Medicean places.

The interest aroused in the lunettes has meant that the fourteen existing canvases from an original nucleus of seventeen which, in 1980 were still divided between the museum "Firenze com'era" and the Palazzo Pitti storerooms, have been brought together and are now all exhibited in the museum "Firenze com'era".

The day when the Medici villas (rightly defined as "the wonderful galaxy surrounding the court at Pitti") manage to recuperate their historical image of splendid places for the journeys, holiday resorts, entertainments and predilection for collecting things of three royal dynasties (from the Medici to the Lorraines and to the Savoys), the scholars and officials of the Florentine Superintendency may consider accomplished their lengthy work of study, restoration and re-positioning of the scattered collections and furnishings that has been carried out in recent years.

The lunettes that Giusto Utens created for 'La Ferdinanda' of Artimino, that most elegant and modern of the Medici villas, are a fundamental part of the history of Medicean architecture and the Tuscan landscape. With the charm of their narrative painting and by showing us in detail the architecture, parks, gardens and grottos, the rides by coach and on horseback, the games and hunts, in a lively, simple and refined manner they bear witness to the life that went on in the villas owned by the Medici family at the end of the sixteenth century.

d.m.

INTRODUCTION

The series of fourteen lunettes which, in part, are on display at the Topography Museum "Firenze com'era" was commissioned by Grand Duke Ferdinand I for the reception hall of the villa at Artimino. It represents the only complete collection witnessing the considerable consistency of the villas which made up the landed property of the Medici dynasty at the end of the sixteenth century.

For years the lunettes have been considered as the most valid starting point from which to make a historical and structural analysis of the architectonic edifices which were the Medicean villas. The importance of the documentary value that they constitute individually has always forced into second place the intrinsic value of the whole collection as exemplifications of the portrayal of landscapes which corresponded to the descriptive taste of the times.

These portrayals by Utens are typical of the type of landscape painting in which Flemish artists were specialised already in the sixteenth century. The landscape artists of that period used to work at their paintings in their studios, allowing a sufficient freedom of form regarding the topographical views to enable their adaptation to personal interpretations. Utens, however, when having to paint documentary panoramas true to reality, used a cartographer's technique; he started with a survey of the land and architecture, so he would leave his studio, returning in order to reconstruct the image of the whole, which he represented faithfully down to the last detail - though with a free hand regarding the composition. Consequently, the architecture of the buildings and the layout of the surrounding land were reproduced exactly, whilst the perspective was at times falsified so as to show in just one picture all areas of the property, including those which in reality the eye would not be able to take in. Furthermore, the type of vegetation certainly appears reconstituted by the artist's brush: all the trees, whether holm-oaks or cypresses, appear the same, and the different field crops are not distinguishable, unlike the works of Buonsignori who, in his plan of Florence in 1587, defined every kind of tree and crop characteristic of each part of the city.

The survey probably had two separate parts: once he had chosen a central, raised, perspective view-point - such as an onlooking hill or even (in some cases) the roof of the villa in question - he drew the profile of the land which made up the estate, then into this landscape he inserted the architectural plan of the villa and its outbuildings, accurately plotted separately. In this way he obtained a "bird's eye view" perspective. Utens did not always strictly follow the rules of perspective, as for example in the Pitti Palace lunette, where, probably for descriptive reasons, he inserted the Belvedere Fortress in an asymmetry which is completely removed from the geometrical harmony of the context. He took other artistic licences in the Castello and Petraia lunettes, where he cut off the tops of hills thereby making a neat horizontal line, which allowed him to insert a glimpse of sky against which, crowning the whole scene, is silhouetted an orderly row of cypresses. Despite these artificial "adjustments", all the lunettes are strictly faithful to the layout of the country around the villas, to the plans of the villas themselves and to the rules of perspective which govern sight. The only licence of composition is taken in the portrayal of the figures who animate the scene, caught going about their daily business. For years the lunettes were quoted and reproduced without any reference to their author, the exact date or the exact number of the pictures which constitute the complete collection. As recently as 1924, Dami published six lunettes, ignoring the author.[1] In 1931, some of them were exhibited at the Palazzo Vecchio in the "Italian Garden Show" and for the first time the name of the artist and the exact date of production appeared in the catalogue. It was not clear, however, whom we owe this information to, nor which documents were used for reference. In 1933, Bertha Wiles made a brief footnote in her volume "The fountains of Florentine sculptors" where she thanked Giovanni Poggi for kindly having indicated the origin, author and date of production of the paintings, information that he himself had tracked down in a document that referred to the payment made to "a certain" Giusto Utens for some paintings actuated in a room of the villa at Artimino in 1598/99.[2] This revealing document, evidently discovered by Poggi in the course of his studies for the Italian garden show, was never published by him, but the lunettes have subsequently had a definite paternity that has accompanied them in all exhibitions and publications. All the same, we still know very little about Giusto Utens. In 1873 Campori provided a few brief biographic notes (still the only ones we know of) without however making any reference to his paintings. Thus we know that he was born in Brussels and that he settled in Carrara in the second half of the sixteenth century where he got married in 1588; he then became a citizen of Carrara, joined the city's High Magistracy and died in 1609 at Carrara. His son Domenico carried on his father's work.[3]

At last, in 1961, in the margin notes of his article on the villa at Pratolino, Smith published the text of a document concerning the payments made to Utens for his work, probably the same ones that led Poggi to attribute the paintings to the Flemish painter.[4] Then Susan Brown came across new documents in 1970 which threw further light on the execution of these paintings[5], and specifically, brief notes from which we can deduct that the canvases for the lunettes were ready by July 1599; that a month previously Utens had received an advance, but the payment of the 30th August shows that he had not yet started the work as he was busy transferring his family from Serravezza to Florence[6]; that the first payment for finished paintings carries the dates of 18th and 23rd October 1599; that the last payment we know about refers to 1602. We also learn that Utens visited each villa personally to take the measurements of the constructions and surrounding land which he and his assistants needed to accomplish the work.

It is this precision in the architectonic relief that, together with a marked sensitivity to colour, determines the high documentary value of the lunettes. The inventories of the Artimino villa, stored in the *Guardaroba Medicea* section of the State Archives, list seventeen lunettes which adorned the reception hall known as the "hall of the villas". At the moment the complete series consists of fourteen canvases, eleven of which are displayed at the Topography Museum "Firenze com'era" and three are in the warehouses of the Florentine *Soprintendenza ai Beni Artistici e Storici* (ministerial offices of artistic and historical works). Surprisingly, Artimino is missing from the list, the very villa which, on account of it having housed the iconographic collection of the Medici estates on Florentine territory, constituted the ideal centre for the organization of the territorial system. It also represented the synthesis of the political and economic power of the Medici lineage at the time of Grand Duke Ferdinand I.

This iconographic synthesis was apparently mere proof of domination over Tuscan territory through display of relative properties, considering that a typological uniformity does not unite the buildings portrayed. In fact, each villa shows characteristics which differ greatly from one to the other, their having been built for various members of the Medici family over a long period between about 1451 and 1595 and particularly by different architects. It would not therefore be possible with this iconographic collection to establish the concept of the "Medicean villa" in the typological sense, unless one refers each building to its historical moment and the intention of its particular patron. Beyond any stylistic distinctions concerning each construction over the two centuries which determined their typological evolution, the villas were always considered merely a part of the rural property and, moreover, the least essential part. They were simply a part of the estate, or rather the district from which they took their names, as in the case of Cafaggiolo, Trebbio, Poggio a Caiano, Castello, etc. This kind of agricultural enterprise - as common to the rich families of the Florentine *bourgeoisie* as to the ecclesiastical power - was based on the new Tuscan sharecropping relations instituted at the beginning of the fifteenth century. Already since the second half of the fourteenth century the economic reality of the Florentine territory had been that of a group of farms combined with rural buildings which were often correlated to the "country houses" for the owners during holiday-time. It is not clear when the **farm-house** where the occupants were involved in farming became the **country residence** intended as a "place for leisure pursuits" as described in the Decameron of Boccaccio. Neither do we know about the Italian word "villeggiatura" (holiday) when originally there was a term signifying the "otium" and "negotium" of country life. At the end of the fifteenth century agriculture became an educative element even for the learned man and so the ideal of humanism took over in villa life: the synthesis of active and contemplative life.

Machiavelli gaily summarises the entertainments and busy, cultured essence of villa-life in his letter to Francesco Vettori: "I rise in the morning with the sun and go out into a wood of mine which I am getting cut down; here I stay two hours to see over the work of the previous day and to spend some time with the wood-cutters who always have some trouble at hand either among themselves or with the neighbours... After the wood, I go to a spring, and from here to my bird-catching hut. I have a book there, either Dante or Petrarch or one of the minor poets such as Tibullus or Ovid; I read about their amorous passions and their love affairs; I am reminded of mine; I take delight in this thought for a time. I then take myself along the road to the tavern: I talk to passers-by, asking for news of their villages, learning various things, and I note the different tastes and fantasies of men. Meanwhile, lunch-time arrives; with my clan I eat those dishes that my poor estate and scanty means allow. Once I have lunched, I return to the tavern: here I usually find the innkeeper, a butcher, a miller, and two kiln-workers. In this company I fritter away the day, playing *cricca* and tric-trac; and usually this gives rise to thousands of contestations and infinite malice and offensive words fly; and often as not we squabble over money and can be heard shouting even at San Casciano. Thus, surrounded by these lice, I sweep the mould from my brain; and I give vent to the malevolence of my destiny, content that she tread this way to see whether she feels shame at her conduct. Come the evening, I return home to my study; and at the door I take off my filthy, muddy every-day attire, and I put on proper, courtly clothes; then, dressed decently, I enter the court of great men of the past. Here, cordially received by them, I feed on that food which alone is mine and for which I was born; here I am not ashamed to talk to them and ask them the reasons for their actions: and out of their humanity they respond. And, for four hours I feel no boredom; I forget all troubles, I do not fear poverty, death does not dismay me: I transfer my mind wholly to them".[7]

It was in this cultural medium that the first Medicean villas sprung up. They fitted into various principal categories: the castle-villa, originally a stronghold which was transformed by Michelozzi into a "place for leisure pursuits" (the villa of Careggi and - only subsequently - those of Cafaggiolo and Trebbio); the suburban villa, such as Belcanto at Fiesole; the villa having the importance of the "lord's manor", like Poggio a Caiano, which suggests the symbolic taking over possession of the territory. The oldest of the Medicean villas portrayed by Utens - Trebbio and Cafaggiolo - are situated in the Mugello Valley, age-old home of the main branch of the Medici family. These villas were the result of investment by enlarging the agricultural holdings already owned by the family, on consideration of the productive quality of the area. The architectonic scheme developed by Michelozzo in the two constructions appears closed, fenced in, fortified with towers and battlements so that the buildings appear almost isolated from the farming life of the territory. It is evident that the villa was still considered a place of refuge in the face of dangers lurking in Florence, but, however, it still had that aristocratic look which caused Machiavelli to remark that these first two country constructions were "not the residences of private citizens, but palaces".[8]

With the unofficial consolidation of political power, the components of the two branches of the Medici family which descended from Giovanni di Bicci increased their possessions around the city. The purchases of Castello by the side-branch headed by PierFrancesco and of Poggio a Caiano by the one led by Lorenzo the Magnificent were made in the second half of the fifteenth century. The criteria dictating the choice of the place for investment changed, as did the way in which it was intended to make use of the new properties and their relevant buildings. The agricultural element still played a predominant role in the plans for Poggio a Caiano; the villa was to rise in the centre of an efficient farm, with prolific lands and well-cultivated fields.

Giuliano da Sangallo, who was commissioned to supervise the work, created a building with a new typology, marking the change from a gentle-folk's rustic residence to an "old style" house. In the immediate neighbourhood of the villa, Sangallo himself constructed a farm-house, which was the true agricultural centre of the estate, of appearance well above that of a common farm. The two principles which lie at the base of the humanistic concept of life in the country - the *otium* and the *negotium* are thus separated and exemplified in two very distinct architectonic structures.

At the end of the fifteenth century the Medici were already land owners on a big scale. The phenomenon of investment in landed property was common to all the rich Florentine merchant families. They poured their liquid capital salvaged from the bankruptcies of the Northern European banks into the purchase of farms equipped with those structures which form the basis of food production, such as farm-houses, woods, fields, furnaces, stables for the change-over of post-horses. This phenonemon occurred in other parts of Italy as well. Numerous literary sources tell us that a spirited exchange of opinion took place between land-owners on this subject; Heyndenreich quotes the exchange of letters between Fra Agnolo Tovaglia, responsible Mantuan affairs in Florence, and Francesco Gonzaga, to whom Tovaglia sent the plans of his villa which had been drawn up by Leonardo da Vinci, from which the Duke could get ideas for a villa of his own.[9]

Cosimo, first Grand Duke of Tuscany, inherited from the two branches of the Medici family a considerable amount of landed property which he increased by further investment: he bought the villas of Petraia and Topaia; he built the villa of Serravezza in Versilia; he began constructing the mansion at Cerreto Guidi; he restored Careggi and Castello; he confiscated from the Salviati family the palace just outside the city walls known as Poggio Baroncelli (later Imperiale); and, finally, in the city itself, he transformed the Pitti Palace into a ducal residence. Elenora of Toledo, Cosimo's wife, also showed much interest in land investment: in 1548 she bought the estate of Castagnolo on the Pisan plain; in 1549 she obtained the Bibbiena estate on long lease and in 1550 the one at Campiglia, both in the Maremma district; she founded another estate at Massa Maritima; and then in 1558 she acquired from the Piccolomini family of Siena both the large estate of Castiglione della Pescaia and the island of Giglio. These were mostly properties lying on swamps or woodland which needed a considerable reclamation effort before becoming exploitable; a lot was left unmodified and turned into hunting reserves. Indeed Spini observed that in the second half of the fifteenth century the best estates were in the hands of the age-old Florentine families, and the villas and farms that Cosimo I confiscated from them (on accusing them of political misdemeanours) were awarded to those who had served faithfully. Furthermore, besides ensuring the personal domination over large areas of the Grand Duchy, the swampy lands managed to provide a sizeable income from fishing, as this practice could not be carried out in the Tyrrhenean Sea infested by Turks. Besides also the supplying of cities with fish from the sea was long and difficult.

While still a prince, Francesco I followed the paternal plan of land and building investments; he constructed the villas of Pratolino and Marignolle, he purchased the villas of Magia and Lappeggi. His second son, Cardinal Ferdinando, completed the arrangement of villas throughout the territory when he built the villas of Montevettolini and Artimino on the Alban hills. He also enlarged Castello, Petraia and Ambrogiana. To make an analysis of the Medicean villas of the *cinquecento,* one must cast an eye over the rest of Italy, where huge building developments were taking place in that period. From the typological aspect, one can observe two extremely noteworthy phenomena. First, the recreation of the antique Roman villa, such as in the plan of Raphael's *Villa Madama,* where the artist himself declared in a letter that the leitmotif was the "imitation" of an antique Roman villa[10]. Then we have the phenomenon of the Venetian villas which took shape in the late sixteenth century. The distinctive character of this second type of construction is determined by the fact that the villa proper, home of the lord and master and main part of the whole complex, was generally connected to the outbuildings used in farming, such as the stables and the granaries, thus forming an architectonic whole. The Tuscan villa of the sixteenth century was linked to the Roman monumental model which completely eliminated the agricultural component - relegated to secondary architectonic structures at a distance from the principal construction - and attributed the essential part to extensive gardens and parks. In fact we can see from the restructuring of the Castello villa and from the rearrangement of the Pitti Palace as a ducal residence that Cosimo I's main concern was turning the surrounding land into parks and gardens. The mannerist taste of the architects who staged the court pomp and array was applied to the layout of the land around, turning with extreme flexibility and skill from images in wood, canvas, chalk and papier mâché to schemes using greenery, concretions in pomice-stone, sponge, shell and mother-of-pearl. Tribolo, Giambologna, Vasari and Ammannati were the creators of these gardens which constitute a reference point, the foundation for the ensuing development in garden art in Florence and Europe. One of the dominant motives, the most original and sumptious in such splendid, natural scenery, is the system of fountains and the connected play of water. Water has always been a problem for Florence and the whole plain surrounding her; in fact the city has no fountain of mediaeval date as water has always been such a precious commodity. It is significative that the moment Cosimo I siezed power in the city, he proclaimed a competition to have a big fountain built in the Signoria Square, at the corner of Palazzo Vecchio, in celebration of the event. To get water to the fountain it was necessary to build an aqueduct specially, and this was fed by the spring known as Ginevra, a mile outside the San Niccolò Gate. For the fountains of the garden of the Castello villa it was also necessary to install hydraulic rams to channel the water from the Castellina and Petraia springs. Fountains, choreographic water-movements, fish-ponds and hatcheries were thus conceived so that, with this rich iconography, the power of the Medici dynasty could be celebrated. For the entire second half of the sixteenth century the garden was an essential element in the Medicean villa complex, but it was to be transformed, following the tastes of the new court architects. The Pratolino gardens do not allow the visitor to have at one glance a global vision of the architectonic design. The early *cinquecento* "architectonic garden" then became the "garden of the senses", prelude to the baroque taste of the seventeenth century. Once the circle of the family's land possessions on grand duchy territory had closed, the construction of new villas or the restructuring of old buildings was dictated by aims and purposes which were completely different from those that had given rise to the fifteenth-century villa. The new objective of celebrating the family's political power was added to the economic reasons; the importance of productive investment in the land was completely detached from the architectonic value of the building at the centre of the property. The Marignolle, Lappeggi, Pratolino, Montevettolini and Ambrogiana villas were, respectively, suburban residences, places for leisure pursuits and rest stages on the journey between one estate and the next; the farm with all its agricultural annexes was at this point totally removed from the architectonic structure of the villa, which served to make the princely power visible throughout the territory. The villa, taken as a whole with the surrounding lands, was the element of visual organization of the landscape itself.

By the time of Ferdinand I, the land possessions were joined one to another in an unbroken chain; each member of the still numerous family owned, on this territory, his own representative space of self-celebrating importance, consisting of an architecture with formal values with conforming to the institutional power that was the absolute principality. Depending on the hunting season - that is, whether it was to be practised in fen or wood - Grand Duke Ferdinando moved from one area of Tuscany to the other, staying at the numerous villas scattered over the whole territory. The whole court apparatus went with him. This movement between the valley and the hills traced a series of established routes in which the villas had the function of resting places, while at the same time they were ducal residences. Numerous letters by the hand of the Grand Duke himself witness these movements: "... here at Leghorn, from where we, stationary for a few days, will leave, as is our custom, for

Pisa and Seravazza on our usual yearly outings"[11]; "The mail sent from your district was forwarded through Rome by Mail-Coach and arrived when I was out of Florence at my villa at Poggio, and I came here afterwards as I am wont to do now, moving between my estates and following the hunting facilities..."[12]; "During the winter, besides my past-time of hunting, I wander around my country abodes, considering that the air in this season is not like in the city, and I get further and further away just following the hunt until I find myself after Christmas at Pisa, where the air is milder... and, with the hunting seasons over, I spend the New Year at Pisa..."[13]. The members of the court regulated official government commitments in accordance with these movements, keeping in contact by means of an intense, continual correspondence between the secretaries of court and the government secretaries remaining in the city. Diaries were also kept, as, for example, those by Tinghi and Andrea Cioli who recorded thus these seasonal movements: "Their Highnesses went into the country, lunched at Poggio, and from there visited Magia, then Montevetturini and finally, Pisa..."[14]. Everything had to be kept at the ready in Florence so that a considerable number of people and horses could leave at any moment.

For local on-lookers and those who took part in these transfers, these parades of carts, horsemen and wagons loaded with hunting trophies must have seemed the removal of a whole city household into the country. From the correspondence between Ferdinando and his secretaries, it is possible to retrace the movements of the Court in each period of the year[15]. From late summer to early autumn, the court stayed in the cooler zones of Pratolino, Cafaggiolo and Trebbio; when the supplies of game were exhausted, they all returned to Florence, from there moving on up north or to the west, to the large territory that made up the Royal Reserve, the private hunting ground of the Grand Duke which included the villas of Poggio a Caiano, Artimino, La Magia, Ambrogiana, Cerreto Guidi and Montevettolini. When the cold weather arrived, the court moved to the seaside where the climate was more temperate. Ferdinando and his court passed the period from Christmas to Carnival moving from Pisa to the villa of Seravezza or else to the estate of Colle Salvetti and the city of Leghorn. Along the return route to Florence - whether overland or by the River Arno - the group stopped at the villa of Ambrogiana until late spring, as the air by the river was still quite cool and healthy. Then they sometimes stayed at Artimino in the month of July. The villas of Careggi (at this point out of the grand duke's favour and therefore not much used), Petraia and Castello were not included on these journeys as they could easily be reached from Florence. In fact they were really family villas, where the grand dukes were brought up and where the grand duchesses lived when not at court. It was easy to spend a day or afternoon there, returning to the city for the night, so probably it is for this reason that these movements were not mentioned. Neither were the villas of Lappeggi and Marignolle included on these journeys, but then they were not really court residences, belonging as they did to Don Antonio, son of Francesco and Bianca Cappello. The importance of the villa at Artimino must be considered within the context of the movements which constituted life at court. There was a practical reason, it being a new rest point which facilitated the move from Poggio a Caiano to Ambrogiana, and it offered a new access to the Royal Hunting Reserve for the villas of Magia and Montevettolini. There was also, however, a symbolic reason, inasmuch as it was situated on Mount Albano, in the heart of a wide area of Medici property, and thus was the link, both real and symbolic, between the villa and the two valleys. The iconographic collection of Utens' lunettes confirms that Artimino was thought of as the ideal centre of the territorial array of villas.

Daniela Mignani

Notes:

1 - L. DAMI, *Il giardino italiano,* Milan 1924.

2 - BERTHA WILES, *The fountains of Florentine sculptors and their followers from Donatello to Bernini,* London 1933, note 2.

3 - G. CAMPORI, *Memorie biografiche degli scultori, architetti, pittori nativi di Carrara,* Modena 1873, p. 369.

4 - W. SMITH, *Pratolino,* in: *Journal of the Society of Architectural Historians,* XX, 1961, p. 155, note 7.

5 - S. BROWN, *The Medici Villa at Artimino,* unpublished thesis on graduating as Master of Arts, August 1970, examining tutor G. Fanelli, registered at Villa Schifanoia, Graduate School of Fine Arts, Florence.

6 - 26th June 1599 "To Giusto, Flemish painter, twelve (lire)... on account for paintings of all the villas of His Highness'. Government Archives of Florence *Guardaroba* nr. 214, c. 24r *(cf.* S. Brown).

- 4th September 1599 "To Master Giusto Utens, Flemish painter, 30 *denaros* in coins on account for several paintings that he will carry out for the lunettes of the big hall at Artimino or by commission for His Serene Highness, plus six *denaros* to buy various colours... and 90 *denaros* to bring his family from Seravezza to Florence" Government Archives of Florence *Possessioni* nr. 4437 c. 79r *(cf.* Smith and Brown).

- 23rd october 1599 "To Giusto, Fleming, for several paintings of hamlets carried out for the lunettes of the big hall at Artimino" Government Archives of Florence *Possessioni* nr. 4437 c. 92r *(cf.* Smith and Brown).

- 20th November 1599 "Master Giusto, Flemish painter, has finished two semi-circular paintings for the lunettes of the Artiminian hall and to settle his account he has asked for fifteen lire each painting, and on request of His Serene Highness, Passigniani has estimated their value in ten lire each, but on being told this Giusto said that he did not wish to work any more for such a sum which amounts to 20 lire for the two completed paintings, and having had 40 lire on account, of which 30 were on commission of His Serene Highness for the family and 20 to supply colours, so that he is in debit for 20 lire, but he expects to be retributed for the visits he has made to the villas in order to draw up the plans from which other painters will be able to carry out further paintings. He added that he has had lodging at Pitti and board in the dining hall, however he wished to point out his situation to His Serene Highness so that he may do what he pleases. Florence, 20th day of the ninth month 1599". Government Archives of Florence *Mediceo* nr. 1269 (this document was referred to but not transcribed by Brown).

- 22nd June 1601 Giusto, Flemish painter, 8 lire. Government Archives of Florence *Guardaroba* nr. 232, p. 6.

- 1602 Giusto, Flemish painter, 20 lire. Government Archives of Florence *Guardaroba* nr. 233, p. 4.

7 - N. MACHIAVELLI, *Lettera del 10 dicembre 1513,* in: "lettere" ed. F. Gaeta, Milan 1961.

8 - N. MACHIAVELLI, *Istorie Fiorentine,* in "Opere complete", Florence 1843.

9 - L.H. HEYDENUEICH, *La villa: genesi e sviluppi fino al Palladio,* in *Bollettino C.I.S.A.* Andrea Palladio, Xl, 1969, p. 11/23.

10 - P. FOSTER, *Raphael on the villa Madama,* in: *Röm Jahrb. F. Kunstgeschichte, Vienna 1967/68.*

11 - 8th March 1597, from Leghorn to Marquis Groppoli. Government Archives of Florence *Mediceo* nr. 291 cc 150v and 151r *(cf:* Brown).

12 - 6th December 1597, from Ambrogiana to Monsignor di Porzia. Government Archives of Florence *Miscellanea Medicea* nr. 165 insert 10 *(cf.* Brown).

13 - 21st December 1601, from Montevettolini to Cardinal Farnese. Government Archives of Florence *Mediceo* nr. 296 *(cf* Brown).

14 - 18th December 1604, Government Archives of Florence *Miscellanea Medicea*

nr. 165 insert l0: "Diary kept by Cavaliere Andrea Cioli acting as secretary to His Serene Highness from 15th May 1604 to 12th october 1605".

15 - ANDREA CIOLI, *op. cit.;* Piero Usimbardi *Istoria del Gran Duca Ferdinando I* ed. G.E. Saltini in *Archivio Storico Italiano,* Series IV; V-VI, 1880. (Usimbardi was secretary to Ferdinando during the period when he was a cardinal, from 1564 to 1587; he continued in this position until 1591 even after Ferdinando became grand duke); Cesare Tinghi, *Diario di Ferdinando I, granduca di Toscana, scritto da Cesare Tinghi suo ajutante di camere da 22 luglio 1600 sino a 18 settembre 1615,* Central National Library of Florence Codice Gino Capponi 261.

GENERAL REFERENCES:

Il potere e lo spazio. La città del Principe. Exhibition catologue, Florence 1980.

M. Fagiolo, *La città effimera e l'universo artificiale del giardino,* Rome 1980.

A. Godoli, A. Natali, *Luoghi della Toscana Medicea,* Florence 1980.

Il giardino italiano, problemi di indagine. Fonti letterarie e storiche. Proceedings of the Study Congress, Siena, San Quirico D'Orcia. Florence 1981.

M. Mastrorocco, *Le mutazioni di Proteo. I giardini medicei del Cinquecento,* Florence 1981.

Giardini italiani. Note di storia e di conservazione, edited by M.L. Quondam and A.M. Racheli, Quaderno n.3 dell'Ufficio Studi del Ministero per i Beni Culturali e Ambientali, Rome 1981.

E. Wharton, *Ville italiane e loro giardini,* Florence 1983.

A. Conti, *I dintorni di Firenze,* Florence 1983.

Il paesaggio riconosciuto. Luoghi, architetture e opere d'arte nella provincia di Firenze, Catalogue edited by the Provincial Administration of Florence, Florence 1983.

A. Borsi, G. Pampaloni, *Ville e giardini,* Novara 1984.

La fonte delle fonti. Iconologia degli artifizi d'acqua, catalogue edited by A. Vezzosi, Florence 1986.

Il giardino d'Europa, catalogue edited by A. Vezzosi, Florence 1986.

Il giardino romantico, catalogue edited by A. Vezzosi, Florence 1986.

Arte delle Grotte. Per la conoscenza e la conservazione delle grotte Artificiali,

Conference Proceedings, Florence 17 June 1985, edited by C. Acidini Luchinat, L. Magnani, M.C. Pozzana, Florence 1987.

Il Giardino Storico. Protezione e restauro, Proceedings of the Sixth International Colloqium on the Protection and Restoration of Historical gardens, organised by the International Committee of Historical Gardens ICOMOS-IFLA and by the Tuscan Regional Authority, Florence, 19-23 May 1981, Florence 1987.

L. Zangheri, *Ville della Provincia di Firenze. La città*, Milan 1989.

M.C. Pozzana, *Il giardino dei frutti. Frutteti, orti, pomari nel giardino e nel paesaggio toscano,* Florence 1990.

Boboli 90, Proceedings of the International Study Congress for the Protection and Exploitation of the Garden, Florence 9-11 March 1989, edited by C. Acidini Luchinat and E. Gerbero Zorzi, Florence 1991.

C. Conforti, *Iconografia storica delle ville medicee negli archivi italiani ed europei,* in: *Il Disegno di Architettura. Bollettino d'informazione,* n.3, April 1991, Milan 1991, pp.61-65.

L'architettura di Lorenzo il Magnifico, Exhibition Catalogue, Florence 8 April-26 July 1992, edited by G.Morolli, C.Acidini Luchinat, L.Marchetti, Milan 1992.

C. Cresti, *Civiltà delle ville toscane,* Florence 1992.

G. Trotta, *Ville fiorentine dell'Ottocento*, Florence 1994.

Giardini Medicei. Giardini di palazzo e di villa nella Firenze del Quattrocento, edited by C.Acidini Luchinat, Milan 1996.

M.C. Pozzana, *Giardini storici. Principi e tecniche della conservazione,* Florence 1996.

M. Zoppi, *Guida ai giardini di Firenze,* Florence 1996.

P. Maresca, *Boschi sacri e giardini incantati,* Florence 1997.

G. Gobbi Sica, *La villa fiorentina. Elementi storici e critici per una lettura*, Florence 1998.

Giardini storici. Giornata Europea del Patrimonio.19 settembre 1998, Roma 1998, edited by the Ministero per i Beni Culturali e Ambientali and the Associazione Dimore Storiche Italiane.

Artifici d'acque e giardini. La cultura delle grotte e dei ninfei in Italia e in Europa. Proceedings of the Fifth International Conference on Historical Gardens and Parks., Florence 16-17 September 1998, Lucca 18-19 September 1998, edited by I. Lapi Ballerini and L.M. Medri, Florence 1999.

Region of Tuscany, *Giardini di Toscana,* Florence 2001.

M.C. Pozzana, *I giardini di Firenze e della Toscana,* Florence 2001.

I. Lapi Ballerini, *Le ville medicee,* Florence 2003.

Cafagiolo
Tempera on canvas, 1.40x2.41 m.
Florence, Gallery warehouse inv: 1890 nr. 6315
In storage at the Topographical Museum *Firenze com'era*

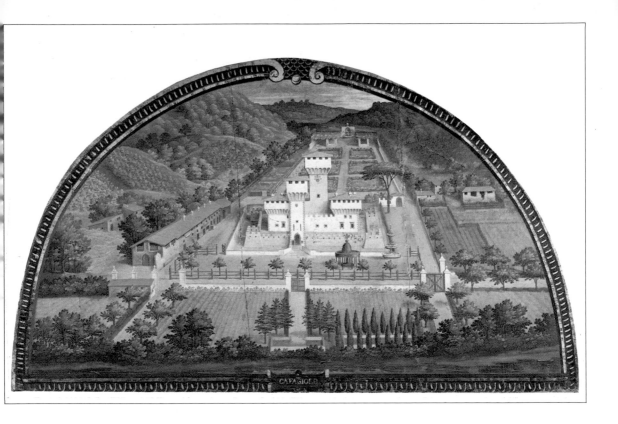

CAFAGIOLO

Il Trebbio
Tempera on canvas, 1.43x2.42 m.
Florence, Gallery warehouse inv: 1890 nr. 6326
In storage at the Topographical Museum *Firenze com'era*

IL TREBBIO

Poggio
Tempera on canvas, 1.41x2.37 m.
Florence, Gallery warehouse inv: 1890 nr. 6323
In storage at the Topographical Museum *Firenze com'era*

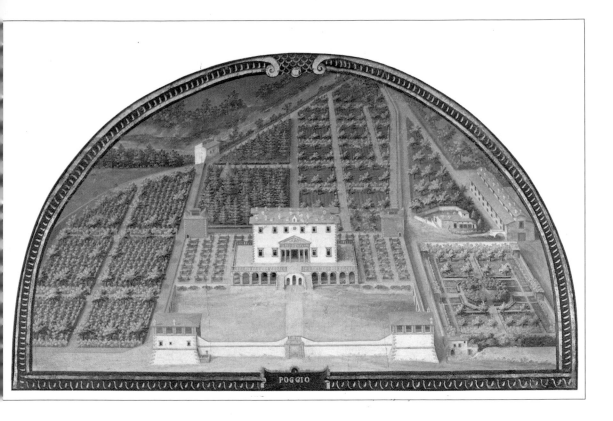

POGGIO

Castello
Tempera on canvas, 1.41x2.33 m.
Florence, Gallery warehouse inv: 1890 nr. 6316
In storage at the Topographical Museum *Firenze com'era*

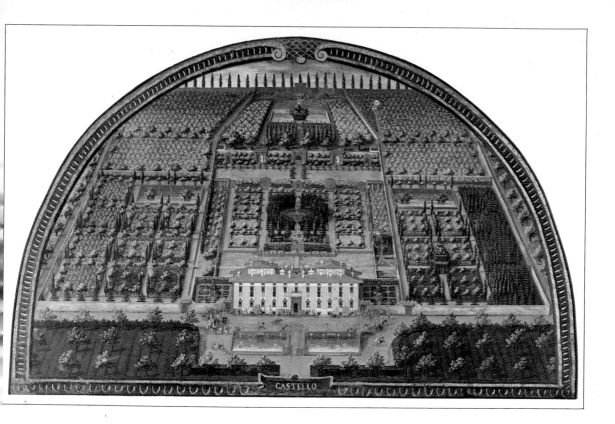

Seravezza
Tempera on canvas, 1.39x2.42 m.
Florence, Gallery warehouse inv: 1890 nr. 6325
In storage at the Topographical Museum *Firenze com'era*

SERRAVEZA

La Petraia
Tempera on canvas, 1.37x2.30 m.
Florence, Gallery warehouse inv: 1890 nr. 6322
In storage at the Topographical Museum *Firenze com'era*

LA PRETAIA

Belveder con Pitti
Tempera on canvas, 1.43x2.85 m.
Florence, Gallery warehouse inv: 1890 nr. 6314
In storage at the Topographical Museum *Firenze com'era*

BELVEDER CON PITTI

Pratolino
Tempera on canvas, 1.45x2.45 m.
Florence, Gallery warehouse inv: 1890 nr. 6324
In storage at the Topographical Museum *Firenze com'era*

PRATOLINO

La Peggio
Tempera on canvas, 1.43x2.38 m.
Florence, Gallery warehouse inv: 1890 nr. 6318
In storage at the Topographical Museum *Firenze com'era*

LA PEGGIO

La Magia
Tempera on canvas, 1.41x2.40 m.
Florence, Gallery warehouse inv: 1890 nr. 6319
In storage at the Topographical Museum *Firenze com'era*

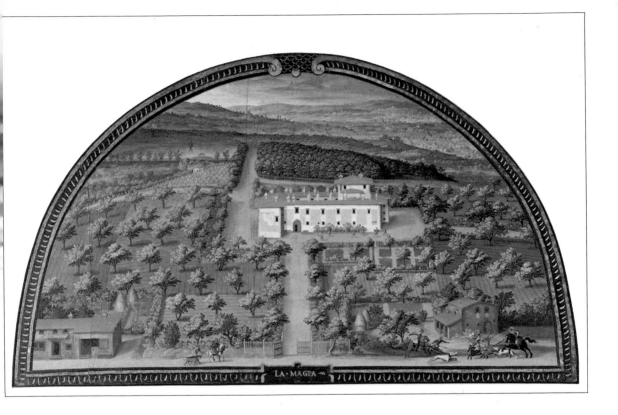

LA·MAGIA

Marignolle
Tempera on canvas, 1.40x2.44 m.
Florence, Gallery warehouse inv: 1890 nr. 6320
In storage at the Topographical Museum *Firenze com'era*

MARIGNOLLE

L'Ambrogiana
Tempera on canvas, 1.44x2.39 m.
Florence, Gallery warehouse inv: 1890 nr. 6313
In storage at the Topographical Museum *Firenze com'era*

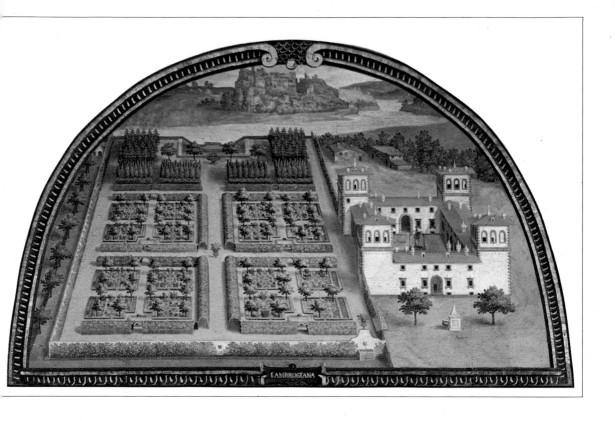

L'AMBROGIANA

Monte Veturino
Tempera on canvas, 1.43x2.43 m.
Florence, Gallery warehouse inv: 1890 nr. 6321
In storage at the Topographical Museum *Firenze com'era*

MONTE VETVRINO

Colle Salvetti
Tempera on canvas, 1.44x2.35 m.
Florence, Gallery warehouse inv: 1890 nr. 6317
In storage at the Topographical Museum *Firenze com'era*

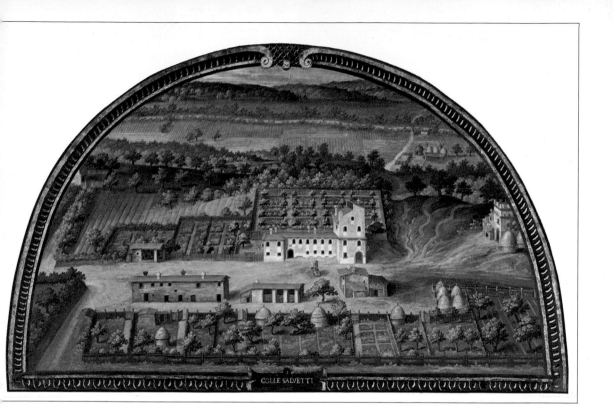

COLLE SALVETTI

Cafagiolo

The villa is situated to the north of Florence, in the Mugello Valley, original age-old home of the Medici family. The property dominated a vast area, protected in the west by a series of hills and surrounded by fields extending to the Sieve.

The original lay-out of the villa dates back to the fourteenth century, when it was a Republican fortress. On becoming Medici property, it was turned into a country residence. In 1427 the Land Registry Office described Averardo de' Medici's property as a "residence functioning as a fortress" with a moat and also "a house detached from the afore-said location, with family abode and stables". In 1451 Cosimo the Elder commissioned Michelozzi to transform the ancient manor-house into a residential building. In the inventory of the assets that Piero de' Medici owned in the Mugello Valley in 1468 after his father Cosimo's death, the property is described as it was in that period, with the transformation by Michelozzi terminated: "A large dwelling built in the manner of a fortress, with a walled moat around it, and with internal walls beyond that, and with two towers containing 4 dovecots, and other edifices according to what one would expect from such an abode, situated in the township of San Giovanni a Petrojo, known as Cafaggiolo, overlooking a large square, walled in on two sides, and on the other more walled dwellings behind a long, straight wall serving the needs and convenience of such dwellings (or rather fortress) that is, having sheds and stalls and wine cellars and four houses for habitation, that the afore-said walled square with these dwellings surrounds the afore-said stronghold (or rather abode) on three sides and behind it there is a vegetable garden of about four bushels, walled on three sides and on the other fenced. We keep this for our residence, together with the annexed implements that one would expect for our needs and for the convenience of our possessions in the Mugello. A furnace for building materials, called the furnace of Cafaggiolo, from which we make some fixed profit, as appears from the written agreement which we confirm in venerable memory of Piero di Cosimo, but we also take advantage of the better quality obtained through our own fabrication, and with this furnace about 17 bushels of earth pass through our hands". When the line of Cosimo the Elder was extinguished with Duke Alessandro, Cafaggiolo passed with all the family assets to the branch of Grand Duke Cosimo I, who in turn donated the estate to his son Don Piero.

At the death of Cosimo I, the property consisted of 30 small holdings, a mill, nine houses, cottages, an inn, three furnaces and 895 bushels' worth of wooded land. Then, on the death of Don Piero, the villa was transferred to his brother, Cardinal Ferdinando. We can see from Utens' lunette that the villa in Grand Duke Ferdinando's time still corresponded perfectly to the description of 1468. The high towers and fortified walls recall the period when the Florentine political situation made it necessary for the Medici family to have a place offering a safe and self-sufficient refuge in case of trouble, far from the perils of the city. Despite the stern appearance of the construction, Utens managed to convey the tranquil, serene atmosphere of the place in Ferdinando's time. The villa was then at the centre of an enormous game preserve and a very affluent agricultural estate. The construction, closed in by the surrounding valley, overlooked a little garden at the back which was disposed in a series of simple beds. Flanking the villa on the other sides were the farm outbuildings, such as the stalls, the barn and the servants' quarters. Tinghi's diary records that from 1600 to 1607 Grand Duke Ferdinando had the habit of passing the months of September and October at Cafaggiolo, one of his favourites, because it could provide the grand duchy kitchens with everything that was needed. The nearby Sieve produced trout and other fish that the Sire himself fished; the woodlands and forests any kind of game; and the fields excellent wine and fruit of various kinds. During these holiday months, Cafaggiolo became a princely palace visited by ambassadors, cardinals, princes, politicians and couriers bringing despatches from the various principalities throughout Italy. Tinghi also recounts how the Grand Duke used to get up early to go hunting in the woods with the gentry, changing route every day. When he was in the vicinity of Gagliano, he would lunch at the antique villa Ubaldini with the Marquis Del Monte; if he did not venture far away, he would return home for lunch. The days he did not go hunting, he would go fish-netting along the Sieve, sometimes as far as San Piero a Sieve. Other times he used to go out riding or in his carriage to the San Martino fortress, or to the parish churches of Santa Agata or Fagna, to the convent of Bosco ai Frati, or to his cottages at Panna. Country receptions were also held at the villa; "On Sunday, hunting at Trebbio, then, after lunch, held audience with the visitors, then, wanting to please Her Ladyship and

Their Serenities, his sons the Princes, he invited all the young ladies around about Cafaggiolo and gave a dance - with gifts - on the lawn at Cafaggiolo, where His Highness enjoyed himself thoroughly."

The villa remained an autumn holiday resort even for the grand dukes who succeeded Ferdinando.

At the time of the Lorraines, it constituted an intermediary stopping-off point in Peter Leopold's movements between Florence and Tuscan Romagna, and indeed of all illustrious guests descending from the north who were directed to Florence along the new Bolognese postal route, opened up in about 1763.

In 1864 the Italian government put the villa and estate up for auction. They were bought by Prince Marcantonio Borghese, who made substantial alterations to the Michelozzi building that had stood unchanged for centuries.

Circumferential walls were pulled down, the moat filled in, the central tower demolished, and the rooms decorated in an antique style, thus transforming the antique Medicean stronghold into a country villa.

H. Acton, *Ville Toscane,* Florence 1974, p. 14.

G. Baccini, *Le ville medicee di Cafaggiolo e di Trebbio in Mugello,* Florence 1897.

G.M. Brocchi, *Descrizione della provincia del Mugello,* Florence 1748, pp. 49-50.

C. Conforti, *Le residenze di campagna dei Granduchi,* in: *Città, ville e fortezze nella Toscana del XVIII secolo,* Florence 1978, p. 14.

G. Milanesi, *Di Cafaggiolo e d'altre fabbriche di ceramiche in Toscana,* Florence 1902.

F. Niccolai, *Mugello e Val di Sieve,* Borgo San Lorenzo 1914, pp. 345-349.

G. Righini, *Mugello e Val di Sieve,* Florence 1956, pp. 114-118.

Sources

Government Archives of Florence, *Quartiere S. Giovanni, gonfalone Vaio,* file nr. LX, c. 82 and fol. *(cf.* Milanesi, *op. cit.).*

Government Archives of Florence, *Mediceo avanti il Principato,* file nr LXXX, cc. 406/409 *(cf.* Milanesi, *op cit.)*

C. Tinghi, *op. cit.,* 2 ott. 1605 *(cf.* Baccini, *op. cit.).*

Trebbio

Situated on a hill not far from Cafaggiolo, the villa of Trebbio was one of the first properties owned by that most ancient branch of the Medici family who made their first land investment in the area of the Mugello. In 1451 Cosimo the Elder entrusted Michelozzi - then working at Cafaggiolo and at Fiesole - with the task of fitting up the mediaeval construction on the estate as a country residence. Michelozzi transformed the fourteenth century building - all the while keeping its mediaeval flavour - into a villa of simple structure, square-shaped, with a central courtyard and a guard tower; like at Careggi and Cafaggiolo we can find here the covered patrol walk-ways, supported by shelf-like projections, which skirted the building at the top.

The villa was at the centre of a big farming estate divided up into twenty-eight small-holdings, and, together with the lands of the Cafaggiolo estate, they made up a true Medicean fief, covering a large portion of the Mugello. Trebbio was the summer residence of the first Medici generation. Cosimo, son of Giovanni dalle Bande Nere, was here when he heard about the assassination of Duke Alessandro and set off for Florence to seize power in the city. When he became Grand Duke of Florence, he gave the property - consisting, at that time, inasmuch as 40 small-holdings with houses, granaries and other accessories, and 16 peasant houses - to his son, Don Piero. When the latter died without off-spring, the property was taken over first by his brother Francesco and then, on his death, by Cardinal Ferdinando, who further enlarged the property, adding possessions at Barberino, San Piero a Sieve and Scarperia.

The principal structure of the building remained practically unchanged from Michelozzi's transformation up to the time of Ferdinando when Utens portrayed it in his lunette.

The construction rises up at the top of the hill. It looks quite segregrated" but it is not fortified, like the Cafaggiolo villa. A sort of barrier around the large square facing the edifice is made up of a series of farm out-buildings. There is no park but a wood behind the villa, in part closed in by walling and in part by fencing. To the right there is a little garden in the fifteenth century form of "hortus conclusus", enhanced with pergolas and small, well-designed flower beds. The property, encompassed in a small, self-sufficient farming community, is complemented with a chapel for religious services.

Grand Duke Ferdinando was very attached to the estate and never failed to visit it when he was on holiday at Cafaggiolo. Tinghi recalls: "His Highness went to lunch at the villa of Trebbio, a truly beautiful villa, both for the scenic position and the income it brings in, and much more because it was the joy of Grand Duke Cosimo, and here he rests when feeling the strain of the Florentine duchy."

In 1645 Grand Duke Ferdinando II sold the property - which had been further enlarged to include 51 land lots, houses, cattle sheds and cellars - to Giuliano Serragli. This latter, on his death, donated the whole property to the Philippine Fathers of the Oratory of San Firenze, with the commitment to use its income - at that time amounting to 3,000 *scudos* - for the building of the present oratory and annexed building, now seat of the Civil Tribunal. The villa belonged to the Philippine Fathers until 1865, the year that the Italian government deliberated on the confiscation of ecclesiastical assets. On being brought up for auction, it passed into private hands; the Coibrò family bought it first, only to sell it shortly afterwards to Prince Marcantonio Borghese.

The antique building complex has remained practically unchanged: the villa is intact in its original form with its little fifteenth century garden and chapel. Even the buildings surrounding the villa, though modified, have kept the same lay-out. The big, open square facing the villa was, however, transformed into a big park of cypresses in the nineteenth century.

H. ACTON, *op. cit.,* p. 14.
G. BACCINI, *op. cit,* p. 142-145.

Sources
C. TINGHI, *op. cit*, 30 settembre 1603 (*cf.* Baccini *op. cit.*).

Poggio

Designed in 1485 by Giuliano da Sangallo for Lorenzo de' Medici, the fifteenth century villa of Poggio a Caiano constituted a typological example of a princely rural villa for the duration of the *Cinquecento*. Behind the plans of the villa there was an intent and a conception which were different to those inspiring the construction of Villa Medici at Fiesole (1460-1470), intended as a suburban villa, i.e. as a "place for leisure pursuits". From the start, the determining factor in the formation of the Poggio a Caiano estate was farming, concentrated however, into an autonomous group, set apart from the architectonic entity of the villa. By 1470 Lorenzo de' Medici had already acquired vast expanses of land in the area. Sangallo's plans provided for a "noble farm-house" in the immediate vicinity of the villa, rationally structured and constituiting the central organization of the actual farming activity. As can be seen from Utens' lunette, it was built to the right of the villa (the main construction), outside the massive walls which marked the boundary. The villa itself displays characteristics of a new kind of construction, synthetizing the metamorphosis from a "gentleman's" country house to an antique-style villa. The simplicity of the building and its extension in width were traditional components of the Tuscan country house. By contrast, the monumental, arched style of the ground floor on which the villa is built (following the outlines of the antique Roman villa), the regularity of the villa's lay-out, the central positioning of the main hall, the technical accomplishment of the coffered ceilings in the barrel vaults of the vestibule and the main hall, and, above all, the collonade on the façade with its triangular gable borrowed from ancient temples: all are inspired by ancient prototypes, indicating the classical education, rich in archeological references, of an architect of the calibre of Sangallo.

Montaigne, who visited Poggio a Caiano in 1580 during his journey through Italy, wrote in a brief description that the villa had been taken as a model for the constructor of Pratolino: "...Poggio, maison de quoi ils font grand feste, apartenant au duc, assis sur le fleuve Umbrone; la forme de ce bastiment est le modele de Pratolino. C'est merveille qu'en si petite masse il y puisse tenir çant très belles chambres."

Differently to the previous castle villas by Michelozzi, the defensive function was completely removed from the construction and depended on a solid boundary wall that surrounded it at a distance. The Poggio a Caiano complex, while responding to the requisites of a well-defined land investment on a particularly productive area, revealed a new function of properties and their relative buildings. Stripped of any purely practical utility, the villa displays, even in its outward appearance, its real purpose of holiday and resting place, overlooking (as it does) the neat surrounding countryside.

After the death of Lorenzo, the construction of the villa was finished by his son Giovanni, future Pope Leo X, who held a lavish court here. Among the most important works that he carried out one must mention the decor of the central hall with frescoes that allegorically celebrate the gestures of the Medici family. The paintings were begun by Andrea del Sarto (1512) and by Franciabigio (1520), continued by Pontormo (1532) and completed by Allori (1580). Around 1570, at the time of Francesco I, some modifications were made to the villa, the first of which being the remaking of the fortified enclosure wall, carried out by Bernardo Buontalenti in the mannerist fashion we see in the lunette. The suites for Bianca Cappello, future Grand Duchess, were put in order during the same years. After the death of the couple in those very same rooms in 1587, the villa remained one of the most important Medicean properties; it was used particularly as a stop-off point and rest place for illustrious court visitors before their entrance into the city. In 1807 Poccianti designed the semicircular staircase which substituted the original Sangallo stairs at the front appearing in the lunette. In the second half of the nineteenth century it became a holiday home for Victor Emanuel II of Savoy and underwent substantial changes which altered even the internal structures of the building.

H. ACTON, *op. cit,* pp. 282-283.

C. CAROCCI, *I dintorni di Firenze,* Florence 1907, pp. 372-373.

C. CONFORTI, *op. cit.* pp. 14-16-18-19.

G. DE MONTAIGNE, Voyage en Italie par la Suisse et l'Allemagne, Paris 1955, p. 155.

F. FONTANI- A. TERRENI, *Viaggio pittorico della Toscana,* Florence 1801, vol. ll, p. 127.

G.C. LENSI ORLANDI, *Le ville di Firenze,* Florence 1954, vol. 1, pp. 36-41.

G. MARCHINI, *Giuliano da Sangallo,* Florence 1942.

Palazzo Vecchio: *Committenza e collezionismo medicei,* Florence 1980, file nr. 621 edited by D. Mignani.

S. BARDAZZI, E. CASTELLANI, *La villa medicea di Poggio a Caiano,* Florence 1981.

L. MEDRI, P. MAZZONI, M. De Vico Fallani, *Villa di Poggio a Caiano,* Florence 1986.

Castello

The villa is situated to the north east of Florence, on the slopes of Monte Morello. It is the oldest villa property of the Medici, having first belonged in 1477 to Lorenzo di Pierfrancesco, a family side branch. Here Cosimo I de' Medici was brought up, remaining particularly attached to it. In the extensive building programme he promoted, the villa and surrounding territory acquired a position of particular importance. In 1537 he called Tribolo back from Bologna to entrust him with the reorganization of the villa and its connected gardens. The artist's major concern was concentrated on adapting the whole complex to the landscape, rather than dealing with the architectonic block. Benedetto Varchi had drawn up a vast iconographic project for the garden: the fountains and statues were to celebrate the glory of the Medici family, Florence and Tuscany as a whole. Another theme was was the nature cycle, represented under an allegorical guise. This was the first time in art history that such a global plan was at the core of a park lay-out. On carrying out this grand, ambitious project, Tribolo revealed his great gifts not only as sculptor and designer, but also as a technician and hydraulic works expert. In fact Vasari mentions that, in order to provide water for the fountains, water displays and fish ponds, he accomplished, together with Piero di San Casciano, an aqueduct that collected the waters from Petraia and the nearby spring of Castellina.

At the death of Tribolo in 1550, the work was far from completed. Vasari took over the supervision of the restructuring, and won the praises of Baldinucci for complying with Tribolo's original plans. Nonetheless, his original scheme was not carried out in its entirety; Vasari himself, in his biography of Tribolo, says that the enlargement of the villa had been planned, and that from this a long avenue was to lead to the Arno, flanked by "small canals...full of different kinds of fish and shrimps". Vasari also says that if all these projects had been carried out "all these adornments would have made these gardens the grandest and most splendid in the whole of Europe".

The gardens were completed thanks to Bernardo Buontalenti, who worked on the restructuring of the building at Castello round about 1592. The villa overlooked a space divided up by paths running down and across the gardens and diving into grottos; paths which were flanked by hedges or walls, following precise perspective ratios. Nature was totally subordinated to the architecture along regular geometrical shapes; the land was transformed into

terraces, steps and avenues, while the plants were forced to form arches, columns and labyrinths. On portraying the villa as it appeared at the end of the *cinquecento,* Utens gave emphasis to the lay-out of the landscape but, in order to represent the gardens as ideally planned (i.e. as they had been originally conceived), he betrayed his meticulous descriptive accuracy. The artistic licences that the artist took were many. Firstly, he lined up the principal axis of the garden with that of the villa. Secondly, he deformed the perspective so that he could show the whole back garden: as the hill sloped steeply down, a bird's eye view perspective could not have taken in, at one glance, all the fountains on the central avenue, as well as the last garden which contained the Appennino fountain, considerably raised off the ground. Finally, he limited the portrayal of the villa, keeping it closed in within its boundaries and, to crown the whole picture, a horizontal line bearing a row of cypresses (in accordance with the calligraphic mode typical of his painting) cut off the hill top which in reality sloped up to Mount Morello. The depiction of the tournament taking place on the square facing the villa is very pleasing. The packed crowd which looks on is represented in detail; the whole household takes part in the event, the servants even are distracted from their usual tasks, the gardens are deserted and from all the attic windows the profiles of house maids can be made out.

Castello could boast the first Medicean garden the beauty of which was renowned throughout Europe. The Boboli gardens and the Petraia park followed suit, also having in common as their distinctive charateristic the long central avenue which led to just one view-point; a characteristic that we also find successively in the southern park of the Pratolino villa, differing substantially, however, from the earlier ones. Here in fact in the fact that the plans conceived hidden paths, imperceptible on first glance, and the architectonic design was broken up into separate natural entities connected to each other by pure emotions inspired by the natural elements.

From the sixteenth century on, the villa was visited by illustrious people of the period who left behind important descriptions. The French botanist and zoologist Pierre Belon included it in his journey around Mediterranean countries between 1546 and 1549, and accurately described all the exotic plants growing there. The beauty and originality of the plants, as well as the gentle stretch of avenue, also struck De Montaigne when he visited it thirty years later; the construction, on the contrary, did not impress him with its peculiar simplicity.

In fact he wrote in November 1580: "La maison n'a rien qui vaille; mais il y a diverses pièces de jardinage, le tout assis sur la pente d'une colline, en manière que les allèes droites son toutes en pente, douices toutefois et aisèes; les transverses sont droites et unies. Il s'y voit là plusieurs bresseaux tissus et convers fort espès de tous arbres odoriferans, comme cèdres, cyprès, orangiers, citronniers, et d'oliviers, les branches si jouintes et enterelassèes qu'il est aisè à voir que le soleil n'y sauroit trouver entrèe en sa plus grande force, et des tailles de cyprès et de ces autres arbres disposè en ordre si voisins l'un de l'autre qu'il n'y a pas place à y passer que pour trois ou quattre". On his return from Rome, Montaine came back to Florence and again stopped off at Castello; this time he saw the villa in summer whereas the year previously it had been autumn. Though remaining enthusiastic on the whole, he realised that he had imagined the park to be more beautiful in springtime than it really was: "J'èprouvai là ce qui m'est arrivé en beaucoup d'autres occasions, que l'imagination va toujours plus loin que la réalité. Je l'avois vu pendant l'hiver nu et depouillé; je m'ètais donc représente sa beautè future, dans une plus douce saison, beaucoup audessus de ce qu'elle me parut alors en effet".

Cosimo I made the Castello villa his own residence when he retired from public life; he lived here with his second wife Cammilla Martelli and died in 1575. The villa remained one of the most used by the grand dukes and their courts, on account of its off-centre position which at the same time was easily reached from the city. It was thus well looked after; the works of upkeep and of embellishment to the interiors continued till Pietro Leopoldo's government. During the eighteenth and nineteenth centuries some modifications were carried out on both the building and the gardens, but, on the whole, one can say that the villa is one of the best preserved among the Medici villas.

H. Acton, *op. cit.,* pp. 283-284.

C. Carocci, *op. cit.,* vol. I, pp. 286-288.

C. Conforti, *op. cit.,* p. 19.

L. Dami, *op. cit.,* p. 36.

M. De Montaigne, *op. cit..* pp. 87-187.

A. Fara, *L'architettura delle ville bountalentiane nei documenti,* in: *Città ville e fortezze nella Toscana del XVIII secolo,* Florence 1978, p. 29.

C. Fei, *La ville di Castello,* in *L'Oeil,* II, 1967, pp. 56-63.

L. Zangheri, *Le "Piante de' Condotti" dei giardini di Castello e la Petraia,* in: *Bollettino degli Ingegneri,* nr. 2-3, 1971, pp. 19-26.

Quartiere 9, *Castello. Campagna medicea periferia urbana,* introduction by M. Gregori, B.M., La Penna, Florence 1984.

Seravezza

According to local belief, Seravezza, situated near the Tyrrhenian coast in the vicinity of Massa, was originally called "Le Fabbriche" or "The Factories" because it abounded in foundries, forgeries and furnaces for the working of iron extracted from the nearby mines of the Apuane Alps. The community of Seravezza, throughout the fourteenth and fifteenth centuries, was at the core of the battles engaged by the republics of Pisa, Genoa, Lucca and Florence for the possession of Versilia. The community eventually came under the dominion of the Florentine Republic in 1513, awarded by Pope Leo X; from that moment on it shared the destiny of Florence and at the fall of the Republic in 1529 it came under the absolute rule of the Medici dynasty. The entire area had been impoverished by the long struggle, and the activity of transformation of the minerals it was rich in had been interrupted.

In his resolution to reclaim the land and stimulate the economy of the more depressed areas of the Florentine dominion, Cosimo I reactivated the workings of the mines and boosted the activity of marble quarrying. In the valley of Seravezza, the duke himself tracked down the lodes of silver-yielding lead in the Bottino mine, the richest of them all. Benvenuto Cellini recounts in his autobiography that the duke, proud of the minerals extracted from those quarries, gave him several pounds of silver one day and said: "This silver is from my quarries. Make me a nice vase". The grand duke took an interest in all the natural resources of the area and, among these, the excavation of marble was one of the most important. He is traditionally credited with having marketed *mischio,* a type of coloured marble, rich lodes of which were found in the mountains roundabout. In order to encourage and protect this marble excavation, he ordered the exclusive use of Versilian marbles throughout his domains. Galluzzi recalls that for the work on the Pitti Palace "new qualities of marble and quarry stone were extracted from the bowels of the earth, and Seravezza yielded, in particular, *mischios* and statuary which were not inferior to the Carrara quality".

In this area so rich in natural resources, Cosimo I decided to construct a residence of his own, thus affording the combination of the advantages of a pleasant summer stay with the possibility of following closely the work in the mines. The actual building is traditionally attributed to Ammannati; recently,

however, on the basis of stylistic affinities of the villa with the one at Artimino, it has been suggested that perhaps Buontalenti was involved.

The edifice rose out of a large meadow situated between the foot of Mount Costa and the left bank of the River Vezza.

On the death of Cosimo I the building was passed on to his son Francesco I and then Ferdinando I, who made it his summer residence, unhappily neglecting the quarrying activity of the district, which was by now extremely efficient.

The villa was approached along a road that skirted some fields, crossed a bridge over the River Vezza, passed over a fish nursery and arrived in a small square with, on the left, a little vegetable garden closed within its walls and, on the right, the entrance to the villa. Utens had to forfeit representing the front façade of the building in order to depict the estate in its entirety, and so we only see its right face; but we are thus able to see the little chapel behind the villa and the big lawn fringed with trees, opposite which were the stables, joined to the main building by means of a wall skirting the lawn. The villa remained under Medici ownership, even when it was abandoned for a long time. On the extinction of the Medici dynasty it became the property of the Lorraine court.

In 1864 the building was donated by the Italian State to the municipal authorities of Seravezza who first turned it into a prison and then into the Town Hall, which it remains to this day.

L. Bolzano, F. Questa, G. Rovereto, *Guida delle Alpi Apuane,* Genoa 1922, pp. 180-182.

B. Cellini, *Vita.*

A. Dalgas, *La Versilia,* Bergamo 1928, pp. 102-122.

A. Fara, *op. cit.,* p. 27.

G. Galluzzi, *Storia del Granducato di Toscana sotto il governo della casa Medici,* Leghorn 1781, vol. II.

La Petraia

The property came under the Medici family round about 1532 after it was confiscated from the Strozzis by Alessandro de' Medici. In 1568 Cosimo gave it to his son Ferdinando. At that time it was a big agricultural estate producing wheat, oil and fodder.

According to Vasari, Petraia was turned into a rest and leisure home by Cardinal Ferdinando. The work he ordered on it has been attributed to Buontalenti who probably worked here from 1575 to about 1590. The building, then a turreted castle, was transformed in that period into an elegant villa of solid, square structure. The projecting roof had a guard tower at its centre, the only evidence of its ancient medieval existence - accentuated by a protrusion at the top which was supported by a sequence of closely-laid corbels. Utens' lunette illustrates the complex after the architectonic transformations, and this corresponds to its present state. The garden, however, was probably sketched to plan because the pergolas and hedges along the circular paths could not possibly have grown so high at the time of painting. Besides, the pergolas are not present in an etching of the seventeenth century, so it is reasonable to assume that they were never planted. We know definitely, though, that Giulio Parigi worked here in 1631 and 1632 to improve and embellish the villa. Probably the completion of the sixteenth century plan of the park in the present altimetric order is due to him. This layout does not differ much from the late sixteenth century representation by Utens: the uneven slope that surrounded the villa on three sides was transformed into a more even surface articulated in three separate tiers - each one fulfilling a different function of the garden - and joined together by steps. The first tier was the lawn surrounding the ground floor of the villa and was on the same level; adorned with pots of citrus trees and statues, it afforded a view over the hills below, with the River Arno and the city. Down a flight of steps one reached the nurseries, surrounded by animal-shaped topiaries (Utens, though, depicted two flights of steps symmetrically on either side of the nurseries). Finally a double flight of steps led to the gardens, which were divided into eight large beds, some given over to vegetable growing and botanical experimentation. The avenue linking Petraia to the villa at Castello was probably part of the work done by Parigi, but in any case the two properties were already contiguous and formed one large land investment.

During the rearrangement of the Castello gardens in romantic key between 1739 and 1760, Tribolo's fountain was removed to Petraia, together with Giambologna's sculpture which represented Fiorenza wringing her hair.

The park of the villa was opened to the public in 1805, during the Napoleonic period. When Florence became capital of Italy, the villa became the royal palace of the Savoy family. In particular the internal structure of the building was altered on that occasion: the courtyard was covered over with an iron and glass skylight, the terracotta floors were hidden under a Venetian type flooring with stuccoes of imitation marble. On the outside, aviaries were added to the lawn, followed eventually by a small glass belvedere.

E. ACRON, *op. cit.,* p. 284.

C. CAROCCI, *op. cit.,* vol. I, pp. 281-283.

E. Chiostri, *La Petraia, villa e giardino. Settecento anni di storia,* Florence 1972.

C. CONFORTI, *op. cit.,* pp. 20-21.

A. FARA, *op. cit.,* pp. 28-29.

Belveder con Pitti

Luca Pitti's antique mansion was purchased in around 1549 by Eleonora of Toledo, wife of Cosimo I, with the intention of turning it into a residence fit for court. Thus she engaged Ammannati to enlarge the building and Tribolo to landscape the park. At that time Tribolo had already outlined his plans for the Castello villa, but these gardens sprang from a still grander project as he had to create the setting for a royal palace. The artist drew up the plans which are substantially what we still see today, but he died before being able to start on the big venture.

The project was taken on by Ammannati (1560), then Buontalenti (1585), until it was expanded in the seventeenth century by Alfonso Parigi the Younger, who used a landscaping criterion for the area called "dell'Isola". In this way, the gardens were developed with the ingeniousness of four important architects, accustomed to using their creativity in inventing celebration parades and court shows, but who, in this case, operated for the transformation of the hill into a fitting background of greenery for parties and walks.

The fact that the palace with its surroundings is considered one of the "Medicean villas" is confirmation of that peculiar characteristic of the building which, differing from most of the Florentine constructions of that time, suggests its use as an "urban villa" because of its relative off-centre location and also for the importance given to the lay-out of the gardens attached to the palace. It is no coincidence that at the centre of the lunette is placed the Amphitheatre with the Ocean fountain, depicted as it used to appear in the sixteenth century, faithful to Tribolo's plans, before being walled in. The amphitheatre was at the heart of the whole park; it formed the pit for the shows which took place in the open on the stage built on the terrace which closed over the Ammannati courtyard (his fountain was formerly situated here, but was substituted in 1641 by Francesco del Tadda's artichoke fountain), with the palace as a backdrop. Half-way up the hill above the amphitheatre was the fish breeding pond, in the centre of which one can make out Neptune's statue, the work of Stoldo Lorenzi (1565).

For over a century the whole park constituted a vast stage for wedding celebrations, games, balls, masked parades, hunts, tournaments and parties organized by Emilio dei Cavalieri, who was the official superintendent of entertainment.

In the lunette the building is moved completely to the bottom. It was only in the eighteenth century that the façade acquired a scenic effect by means of Ruggieri's gradual architectonic development of the supplementary side wings; in this way the building ended up by occupying the whole hill on which it stood isolated in the *Cinquecento.*

The lunette is closed at the bottom by a horizontal line - the ouline of the Vasari corridor - and on the left one can glimpse the entrance to the Buontalenti grotto.

At the top an artificial axonometry forces the Belvedere fortress into the picture, the Buontalenti building in the centre. On the hilltop to the right, beyond a rampart of the antique city walls that Cosimo I, fearing an attack by the Sienese, had constructed in 1544, one can make out Cavaliere's small house and little surrounding garden, adorned with the monkey fountain by Pietro Tacca. On the other side of the walls which cut the hill longitudinally, the land appears already divided up by Ammannati with his avenues fringed by cypresses and holm-oaks that lead to the Isola nurseries. Next to the city walls on the left, the little Madama grotto can be seen, contiguous to the garden of the same name, the oldest of the Boboli grottoes and the first in chronological order of all those works (grottoes, fountains, sculptures, buildings) which gradually enriched the garden over three centuries.

Government Archives of Florence, *Mostra documentaria e iconografica di Palazzo Pitti e giardino di Boboli,* April - June 1960.

C. CAMBIAGI, *Descrizione del giardino di Boboli,* Florence 1789.

J. CHATFIELD, F. GURRIERI, *Boboli gardens,* Florence 1972.

M. FORLANI CONTI, F. FACCHINETTI BOTTAI, L. BALDINI GIUSTI, *Le mille stanze del Re. Firenze, Palazzo Pitti. Un organismo architettonico e catalogo,* in: *Bollettino d'Arte,* 1, 1979, pp. 79-105.

L. GINORI LISCI, *I palazzi di Firenze,* Florence 1972, vol. II, p. 841.

F. MORANDINI, *Palazzo Pitti, la sua costruzione e i successivi ingrandimenti,* in: *Commentarii,* XVI, 1965, pp. 35-46.

Pratolino

About six miles north of Florence on the road to Bologna, Francesco de Medici purchased, in 1568, a vast land plot with views overlooking Fiesole. The following year, he entrusted Bernardo Buontalenti with the construction of a villa there, complete with a large surrounding park.

During the execution of the work, a crop of panegyric poems celebrated this undertaking by the Medicean prince who caused sensation with the enormous financial commitment and the magnificent extravagance of the project. Gualtierotti wrote in 1579: "Qui l'Arte, e la Natura / Insieme a gara ogni sua grazia porge / E fra quelle si scorge / La grandezza del animo, e la cura / Che le nutrisce, e cura / E fa splender più chiaro ogn'hor d'intorno / Di nuove meraviglie il bel soggiorno". The project took fifteen years; the big park with its gardens was immediately deemed one of the wonders of garden art in Europe. Montaigne, during his journey to Italy in 1580, visited the villa and described it thus: "... un palais que le duc de Florence y a bati depuis douze ans, où il emploie tous ces cinq sens de nature pour l'ambellir... C'est un lieu, là, où il n'y a rien de pleine. On a la veue de plusieurs collines, qui est la forme universelle de cette contrèe. La maison s'appele Pratolino. Le batimant y est mèprisable à le voir, mais de près il est très beau, mais non de plus beaus de nostre France. Ils disent qu'il y a six vingts chambres meublèes; nous en vismes dix ou douse des plus belles. Les meubles sont jolis, mais non magnifiques. Il y a de miraculeus une grotte à plusieurs demures et pieces; cette partie surpasse tout ce que nous ayons jamais veu ailleurs. Elle est encroutèe et formèe partout de certene matière qu'ils disent estre apportèe de quelques montagnes, et l'ont cousue avec des cluos imperceptiblemant. Il y a non sulemant de la musique et harmonie qui se fait par le mouvement de l'eau, mais encore le mouvement de plusieurs statues et portes à divers actes, que l'eau esbranle, plusieurs animaus qui s'y plongent pour boire, et choses samblables. A un sul mouvement tout la grotte est pleine d'eau, tous les sieges vous rejaillissent l'eau aus fesses; et, fuiant de la grotte, montant contremont les echaliers du chateau, il sort de deux en degrès de cest eschalier qui veut donner ce plaisir, mille filets d'eau qui vous vont baignant jusques en haut du logis. La beautè et richesse de ce lieu ne se peut reprèsenter par le menu".

The villa rose out of the crest of the hill, whilst the park unfolded on both sides of the slope below, which was divided into two parts by a wall - the "New Park" situated on the north-facing slope and the "Old Park" on the south-facing slope.

To go from one park to the other one had to cross through the grottoes which were on the level of the ground floor of the villa. The building followed the design of the Poggio a Caiano villa, a princely palace *par excellence*. The central disposition of the building was aligned on a north-south axis; the internal arrangement of the rooms was all based on precise symmetries. Here as at Poggio a Caiano, the main body of the building lay on a "basis villae" which, in this case, was not arches, but a solid wall closing on the inside a series of artificial grottoes: the Grande, Galatea, Stufa, Spugna Bianca, Satiri and Samaritana Grottoes.

The darlings of Florentine artistic culture were called to lay out the gardens, grottoes and fountains: from Giambologna to Vincenzo Danti, from Valerio Cioli to Ammannati. Buontalenti was the inventor of the complex mechanisms that set off the water-works and moving figurations which animated the park. He directed the waters that spouted from the Appennino spring (situated to the north of the "New Park") to the ground rooms of the villa in order to activate the hydraulic bellows which moved the automatons, and then he dispersed them along the numerous pipelines in the park.

Utens' lunette represents the southern view of the villa with below it the "Old Park", the one richer in fountains and sculptures. The painter conceives the body of the building as the culminating element on the hill, as from this stemmed the criss-cross of avenues, paths and streams which shaped the park. Given the steepness of the slope on this side of the hill, a second terrace, designed with a wealth of steps, compensated for the natural difference in level. A wide avenue leading from the villa divided the park exactly into two halves, but beyond the avenue (which was on the same axis as the building) no attempt had been made to organize the garden to a precise architectonic design. This characteristic sets the gardens apart from the preceding Medicean gardens created for the villas of Castello, Petraia and Boboli which were planned in strict symmetry. The terrace by the villa commanded a general view over the lower-lying land - in fact it dominated it - but it was not possible to make out the lay-out of the garden; the visitor was led along laid paths past a profusion of grottoes, statues, streams and labyrinths that joined one point to the next, not shown in perspective, but rather distinguishable only by the perception of the senses - stimulated by a scent, colours, the sound of water or of artificial rain.

In his picture, Utens, however, rationalized this criss-cross of avenues, the hidden paths and the concatenation of fountains, by showing us in perspective that which in reality was distinguishable only through individual perceptions, thus

betraying the mannerist pattern of the Buontalenti garden.

For the foreign travellers arriving from the north, Pratolino, situated on the road to Bologna, was the first of the Florentine wonders. Over the centuries its gardens have been described in travel books; painters and architects have sketched views of the villa and of the park. Only through these descriptions is it possible to bring Francesco I's Pratolino to life. In fact, the water-works and the automatons seemed old-fashioned to seventeenth-century eyes, and little by little the last of the Medici abandoned the pleasures that this villa could offer. When it was transferred to the House of Lorraine, the villa lay abandoned for years. In 1819 the park was transformed into an English garden by the engineer Giuseppe Frichs and the villa - at this point stripped of all furnishings - was completely destroyed in 1822. Some elements of the park have been kept: the web of avenues, the enormous "Appennino" statue, the "Cupid Grotto", the "Fontana delle Maschere", the Chapel and the *paggeria* or courtisans' quarters, which, in the second half of the nineteenth century were turned into a villa following the plans of Enrico Ceramelli and Luigi Fusi, and here the noble Demidoff family lived until the early twentieth century.

H. ACTON, *op. cit.,* pp. 284.

C. CAROCCI, *op. cit.,* vol. I, pp. 204-205.

C. CONFORTI, *op. cit.,* pp. 19-20.

L. DAMI, *op. cit,* p. 39.

A. FARA, *op. cit.,* pp. 28-29.

M. DE MONTAIGNE, *op. cit.,* pp. 82-83.

R. GUALTIEROTTI, *Vaghezze sopra Pratolino,* Florence 1579, p. 10 *(cf.* Zangheri *op. cit.).*

D. HEIKAMP, *Pratolino nei suoi giorni splendidi,* in: *Antichità Viva,* 2, 1969, p. 14.

D. HEIKAMP, *Les merveilles de Pratolino,* in: *L'Oeil,* 1969, p. 16.

F. FONTANI, A. TERRENI, *op. cit.,* vol. VI, p. 131.

W. SMITH, *op. cit.*

L. ZANGHERI, *Per una lettura iconologica di Prafolino,* in: *Antichità Viva,* 4, 1977. L. ZANGHERI, *Pratolino, il giardino delle meraviglie,* Florence 1979.

Several hands, *Il concerto di statue,* catalogue ed. A. Vezzosi, Florence 1986.

Several hands, *Il ritorno di Pan. Ricerche e progetti per il futuro di Pratolino,* catalogue ed. A. Vezzosi, Florence 1986.

La Peggio

The property is situated to the south of Florence, in the neighbourhood of Grassina. It first belonged to the Ricasoli family, from whom Francesco de' Medici, son of Cosimo I, bought it in 1569 and used it as his summer home for some years.

On becoming Grand Duke, Francesco carried out considerable works of embellishment on the whole complex. Under the direction of Bernardo Buontalenti the works took about 47 months, finishing in January 1585. The lunette therefore illustrates the villa during one of its first moments of glory, when it was used as a summer home for the third grand duke of Tuscany and his court.

In the same years, Giorgio Vasari the Younger noted down on the villa plans: "Appeggia, luogo del Serenissimo Gran Duca nell'Antella, intorno al quale rigira il prato ed ha la medesima larghezza, et fuori del palazzo, non molto lontano sono stalle e tinaie grandissime"(*). The main façade of the big building, made up of two rows of porticoes, gave onto a central courtyard enclosed by a crenellated wall with, at the centre, the entrance gate to the villa. The picture that Utens gives us fully reflects the character that, in all likelihood, the enormous complex had in the second half of the sixteenth century: the main building next to its modest garden rests at the centre of the well-cultivated fields which probably made up the sizeable estate. This therefore is a property that summarized the characteristics of land investment and place for leisure, as is witnessed in the painting by the arrival of a coach escorted by horsemen, by the soccer and club-and-ball games going on in front of the villa, as well as by the animated hunting scene in the foreground among the fields.

In 1604 Ferdinando I made over the use of the villa to Count Giovanni Antonio degli Orsini da Pitigliano; in 1640, on the death of Alessandro, last descendant of that particular branch of the Orsini family, it became once again court property. It was assigned in 1667 to Cardinal Francesco Maria, brother of Grand Duke Cosimo III, and with him the most glorious period of the great mansion began. The cardinal had the architect Antonio Ferri practically reconstruct the place and he used it exclusively for grand parties. After his death it was neglected and forgotten, so much so that, put up for auction in 1814, it was in such a poor condition that the new owner, Captain Cambiagi, had to pull down the upper floor and consolidate the rest in order to save at least a part, whilst the park near the villa was transformed into small-holdings. At present, therefore, little remains of the beautiful villa and its garden portrayed by Utens.

*"La Peggio, residence at Antella of His Serene Highness the Grand Duke, surrounded by a lawn of the same width, and not far removed from the villa are stables and enormous wine cellars".

H. Acton, *op. cit.*, pp. 285.
C. Carocci, *op. cit*, Vol. II, pp. 154-156.
A. Fara, *op. cit.*, p. 28.
G.C. Lensi Orlandi, *op. cit*, pp. 87-92.
Palazzo Vecchio: *Committenza e collezionismo medicei,* Florence 1980, file nr. 619 ed. D. Mignani.
G. Vasari il Giovane, *Piante di chiese (palazzi e ville) di Toscana e d'Italia,* Gabinetto Disegni e Stampe di Firenze nr. 4905.

La Magia

The villa is near Quarrata, to the west of Florence, on the northern slope of Mount Albano. The original nucleus of the building consisted of a stronghold constructed by Vinciguerra Panciatichi in 1318, and it was still a fortified construction at the beginning of the sixteenth century when the descendants of Panciatichi took refuge here to escape the magisterial powers of Pistoia. In 1585 the building was bought by Grand Duke Francesco I who engaged Bernardo Buontalenti to turn it into a country residence. The new property bordered on the Poggio a Caiano estate, so the grand duke's purchase can be considered as further expansion of the dominion he already had over the Mount Albano area, by the extension of the hunting grounds of the Royal Reserve instituted by Cosimo I. Buontalenti's work gave a unitary setting to the construction which ended up as a rather irregular structure, square-shaped, with a paved courtyard on the inside. The dove-cot was heightened to make a kind of guard tower on the right corner of the building.

Like all the country villas at the time of the Grand Duchy, the construction is not closed within an external wall, but it looks onto the neat pattern of the surrounding fields. We can also trace back to Buontalenti the organization of the land around the villa, with the wide avenue that leads up to it, circles it and then on the left continues away from it towards the fields. Here it is flanked by a thick wood on the right and on the left by a lake, the walled shores of which were (according to documentary evidence) built under Buontalenti's direction.

Utens' picture was painted just a few years after the conclusion of these works and therefore gives us reliable and detailed evidence of the property as a whole at the time of Ferdinando I.

The land around the villa is shown entirely cultivated; there are no gardens and the villa is separated from the fields only by a vast area open on all four sides. The peasants' houses near the villa and the figures animating the scene characterize the typically agricultural and rural aspect of the estate: gentlemen are playing *palla corda* (a kind of tennis) on the villa forecourt, while in the foreground there is a deer-hunt going on, very like the hunting scene in the lunette of the La Peggio villa.

Hunting as a sport was much practised by Grand Duke Ferdinando, who thus wrote to the Grand Duchess Cristina from Magia: "Today I had a good hunt, and I enjoyed myself tremendously, and I am sending home a triumphant cartload of eleven boars... and because he who kills keeps as trophies the jaws with the teeth, extracted then as you will have seen...". The area, inside the borders of the Royal Hunting Reserve, was obviously very rich in game. One may suppose that Buontalenti's positioning of the lake just behind the villa was because of the fishing it provided, an activity which the Grand Duke often indulged in; the little hut at the centre of the lake appearing in the lunette seems to confirm this hypothesis.

The villa remained the property of the principal branch of the Medici family until 1645, when it was sold to Pandolfo Attavanti. Since then the villa with its appendages has always been private property.

H. ACTON, *op. cit.,* p. 283.
A. FARA, *op. cit.,* p. 28.
G. TIGRI, *Pistoia e il suo territorio,* Pistoia 1834, p. 80.

Sources
Government Archives of Florence *Mediceo* nr. 289, p. 166 v. (*cf.* S. Brown *op. cit.*).

Marignolle

Age-old possession of the Sacchetti family, the Marignolle estate belonged to Lorenzo di Piero Ridolfi in 1550, only to be confiscated a few years later by Francesco de' Medici, on the charge of his having participated in the conspiracy led by Orazio Pucci.

The lunette shows the villa at the time of Don Antonio dei Medici (son of Bianca Cappello), assigned to him in 1587 by Grand Duke Francesco I who had it expressly restored and embellished by Buontalenti.

Marignolle is amongst the more modest of the Medicean villas because it was intended as a gentleman's home, not as a princely palace. The construction, however, is very important from the architectonic point of view inasmuch as it constitutes the intermediate stage in Buontalenti's development between the configuration of the centralised blocks of Pratolino and La Petraia (both in Sangallo's style) and the slender, elongated features of Belvedere and Artimino. The internal distribution is arranged along a longitudinal axis, though at the same time converging on a central nucleus. In this way it determines a horizontal dilatation of the two parallel fronts on the exterior.

Situated at the centre of a vast rectangular lawn, and supported by barbican walls, the villa façade looks out towards Florence.

The courtyard is external to the construction, flanked by a short side that faces an arcade on the ground floor with, above that, a loggia. The crenellated walls fencing in the property confer the traditional aspect of a fortified house.

Around 1621, when the villa together with its farm was returned to the princely court, it was sold by the *Scrittoio delle Possessioni* (Property office) to Piero di Girolamo, descendant of Gino Capponi, and since then it has remained private property, keeping intact its original aspect.

C. CAROCCI, *op. cit.*, vol. II, pp. 372-373.
C. CONFORTI, *op. cit.*, p. 16.
G.C. LENSI ORLANDI, *op. cit.*, vol. II, pp. 264-266.
Palazzo Vecchio: *Committenza e collezionismo medicei*, Florence 1980, file nr. 620 ed. D. Mignani.

L'Ambrogiana

The villa is at Montelupo, at the confluence of the Pesa stream with the Arno. Carocci traces the name "Ambrogiana" back to the Ambrogi family, the first owners of the estate - originally consisting of a little lodge and surrounding farmland - on which the villa was later built.

The actual construction work was due to Grand Duke Ferdinando I; this, in fact, was one of his first building enterprises, as the beginning of the work coincided with his nomination as third grand duke of Tuscany (1587).

Usimbardi, secretary to the grand duke, wrote at that time: "In Tuscany he bought and built on the Ambrogiana just for its convenience on his hunting excursions, and many conveniences there were; in fact, in comparison to the original building, they were increased greatly, as you can see".

It is commonly believed that Buontalenti designed the villa, but this hypothesis, based on a stylistic evaluation of the building, has not so far been proved by documentation. The villa was built on the existing structure overlooking the Arno, and in fact on that side the construction presents an articulation of interior volumes that is different and more complex than the one corresponding on the other side, which is regular.

Utens' lunette was painted shortly after the construction was completed and therefore represents the only known portrayal of the original solid state of the villa as a whole. The building stands on an open space; on the left side there is a sizeable walled garden, which is divided into four geometrical partitions defined by pergolas, the arboreal decorations in vogue at that time and which we also find in the portrayal of the Petraia villa. Behind the garden is a wood of cypresses with a clearing in the centre containing a sunken area with a rectangular stairway and a grotto, the work of Tadda. Fossi has underlined the great originality of inserting a natural element, i.e. the river, in the context of the villa and its garden: the latter extended to the banks of the Arno, which one could reach from a platform constituting a kind of jetty joined to the garden level by steps. The grotto, with its wealth of waterworks, was hewn into the slope coming down from the garden to the river and constituted the ideal mediation between the two natural elements. The villa, on the route linking Florence to Pisa, was for a long time used as a hunting lodge, but primarily it was a resting and refreshment place for the court on its journeys to and from Pisa.

Later, perhaps in the eighteenth century, the construction was completely raised one floor and new windows were opened in the towers, thus altering not only the primitive interplay between full and empty spaces, but also the entire aspect of the building. The view by Terreni of 1801 testifies to the profound transformation undergone by the complex compared to Utens' picture. The court of the Lorraines, while keeping the villa among the properties of the crown, used the place only in passing and less and less frequently. Grand Duke Leopold II had Giuseppe Cantagallina turn it into a mental home round about 1820-22, and it keeps this function to this day.

C. CONFORTI, *op. cit.*, pp. 21-22.

A. FARA, *op. cit.*, p. 28.

F. FONTANI, A. TERRENI, *op. cit.*, vol. IV, p. 255.

M. FOSSI, *Note documentarie sul gruppo di Ercole* e *Anteo dell'Ammannati e sulla villa Ambrogiana*, in: *Architettura e Politica da Cosimo I a Ferdinando I,* ed. G. Spini Florence 1976, pp. 461-479.

Palazzo Vecchio: *Committenza e collezionismo medicei,* Florence 1980, file nr. 618 ed. D. Mignani.

Monte Veturino

The Montevettolini villa, situated on a hilltop of the slopes of Mount Albano, within the territory encompassed by the Royal Hunting Reserve, was built on the initiative of Grand Duke Ferdinando I in 1595 as a resting place for the court during the hunting season.

The estate on which the villa was built already belonged to the Medici family; we know that in 1556 Grand Duke Cosimo I himself stayed at Montevettolini. The architect Gherardo Mechini carried out the construction of the villa which incorporated the structures already existing; a rock and a stretch of wall dating back to the period of municipal government. The result was a building with an extremely irregular format. The right side was three storeys high, incorporating the ancient rock; the left side was situated on lower-lying land, thus having an extra floor, and it was built onto a part of the original wall.

In the spring of 1600, the parish of Montevettolini made over to Ferdinando, for the sum of 40 *scudos,* a piece of land which lay between the villa and the rectory; this purchase, made for the "construction of the villa", shows how the work of enlarging the building continued until the beginning of the seventeenth century. Utens therefore painted his lunette when work was still being carried out on the villa. In this case, the painter limits himself to describing exactly the construction that he had probably seen at the planning stage and not completed. Regarding the surrounding area, instead of emphasizing the elevated position of the villa which allowed it to dominate the whole of the under-lying valley, he lowered the building in the picture by looking down on it from an even higher position, which could have been the top of Mount Albano.

The portrayal of the villa is highly detailed: the construction appears to have kept its aspect of imposing rock, even throughout the late fifteenth century transformations. On the front of the building, the four polygonal watch towers, complete with narrow openings, contribute to confer this impression. Two sides of the villa hung over the valley below, while to the right a small courtyard separated it from the constructions nestling around the ancient hamlet nearby the main façade, meanwhile, overlooked a wide space laid out as a park.

Although it was very imposing, the building never had those architectural and natural requisites which were typical of the villas designed by Buontalenti and Ammannati for Grand Duke Ferdinando. All the same, the latter often went there with his court as, being the villa at the centre of vast Medici possessions in the lower Nievole Valley, it made an important centre for the administration of his agricultural interests.

Tinghi noted in his diary: "Il granduca partì da Montevetturini et andò a vedere le sue posesione dell'aquisto lungo il lago di Fucechio...tutto il giorno Sua Altezza andò rotta a vedere le sudette possessioni con gran suo gusto et utile asaj."(*)

With a rescript dated 17 August 1650, Grand Duke Ferdinando II ordered the sale of two thirds of the property, including the villa.

The estate went to the Bartolommei family, who remained proprietors until 1871, when they sold it to Prince Marcantonio Borghese. The latter carried out extensive restoration work on the building to give it back, where possible, its sixteenth-century character.

(*) - "The Grand Duke left Montevetturini and went to see his holdings purchased alongside the lake of Fucechio...all day His Highness visited these same properties with great satisfaction and utility."

G. BARONTI, *Montevettolini e il suo territorio,* Pescia 1896.

G. BIAGI, *In Val di Nievole,* Florence 1901, pp. 334-336.

D. MARZI, *Notizie storiche di Monsummano e Montevettolini dai documenti dell'archivio comunale nuovamente ordinato,* Florence 1894.

C. STIAVELLI, *L'arte in Val di Nievole,* Florence 1905, p. 132.

Sources

C. TINGHI, op. cit. (*cf.* S. Brown).

Colle Salvetti

The property was situated near the Tyrrhenian Sea on a hilltop of the last western ramification of the lower Pisan hills. It overlooked a great plain that extended down to the sea.

Spini includes Colle Salvetti among the oldest properties of the Medici family. Seemingly it already belonged to them at the time of Cosimo the Elder.

Repetti informs us that, round about 1571, the abbot *in commendam* of the community of Colle Salvetti granted donna Eleonora of Toledo, wife of Cosimo I, perpetual lease of the estate, Abbey property.

This form of donation was probably in addition to other Medici property on the hill.

A few years afterwards, during the time of Grand Duke Ferdinando I, the estate must have held great importance among the Medicean land property holdings, enough for it to be considered worthy of being portrayed in Utens' series of lunettes.

In the painting, the property is shown as a big agricultural estate, consisting of the main building - rustic in character - and numerous farm outbuildings; these were probably the farmer's lodge, sheds for farming equipment, stalls and cellars. It was certainly its geographical position which gave prominence to the estate, with it being at the centre of vast, fertile smallholdings, while, at the same time, it was very close to Leghorn, so that it could be used by the court as a resting place on the journeys between the sea and Florence.

G. Spini, *Architettura e Politica da Cosimo I a Ferdinando I,* Florence 1976, p. 34.
E. Repetti, *Dizionario Geografico, Fisico, Storico della Toscana,* Florence 1833, vol. I, pp. 770-771.

COPIES OF UTEN'S LUNETTES AND FABRICATIONS

The series of paintings had always been part of the furnishings of the Artimino villa, so the owners who took over from the Lorraine family commissioned copies which were exactly true to the originals. These stayed in the "hall of the villas" until 1969, when all the furnishings which had adorned the villa since 1782 were sold at a big auction.

Three other lunettes appeared at the auction to complete the series, but these were painted more recently, probably at the turn of the century.

Unfortunately these three lunettes are not copies of the originals, but are the fruit of fantasy, executed with a technique that suitably aged Zocchi's eighteenth century views. This is recognizable from the eighteenth century type of viewpoint adopted, and it is confirmed by the denomination of the villa of Poggio Imperiale, which, at Utens' time was called "Poggio Baroncelli" (it was only in 1624, with an edict of Maria Magdalena of Austria, that it took on the name of "Poggio Imperiale"). In any case, the choice of the anonymous twentieth-century painter who added the villas of Careggi, Cerreto Guidi and Poggio Imperiale to the incomplete series is not completely unjustified.

These pictures also are part of the Medici family's antique landed heritage and they have the right to complete the summary of the situation of Medici property at the time of Utens.

However, the disappearance of three of the villa lunettes and of the seventeen battle lunettes which decorated the "hall of wars" remains a mystery.

Villa **La Ferdinanda** at Artimino
Hall of the Villas in 1969 at the time the furnishings were auctioned.
Copies of Utens' lunettes on the ceiling

Careggi

The villa of Careggi has been, rightly enough, defined as "the third (chronologically speaking) suburban home of the Medicis", as well as "their favourite", considering that it "joined the mainly rustic characteristics of the villa-cum-farm to the extreme vicinity of the city, with all the advantages of both practical and political natures that such a circumstance allowed" (Conforti).

The castle at Careggi was purchased in 1417 by Giovanni di Bicci, progenitor of the Medici family. It was one of the favourite residences of Cosimo the Elder, who had the Michelozzo building restructured and enlarged. The antique stronghold was transformed into a villa without destroying the original castle outline, maintained in the crenellated gallery that crowns the main body of the building.

Various members of the Medici family frequently stayed at the villa; Cosimo the Elder died here in 1464 and Piero the Gouty in 1469; Lorenzo the Magnificent loved to visit the rooms at Careggi where tradition has it that the celebrated Platonic Academy of Marsilio Ficino gathered.

The villa was set on fire in 1494, when the Medicis were banned from the city during the Republican government with Savonarola (1452/1498) holding the reins. Duke Alessandro de' Medici subsequently had restoration work carried out, which was then completed at the time of Grand Duke Cosimo I, who also had Pontormo and Bronzino fresco some rooms. These embellishments during the sixteenth century did not modify the fifteenth-century stamp of Michelozzi's which stayed unaltered until the nineteenth-century.

Interest in the villa was then lost and in 1779 it was sold to private owners by Grand Duke Peter Leopold of Lorraine.

The property first passed to the Orsi family. They sold it in 1848 to Francis Joseph Sloane, who it is assumed carried out some modifications to the original plan of construction and to the layout of the park (in accordance with the precepts of the nineteenth century). The property changed hands again, first to Count Augusto Boutourlin in 1871, and then to the Hospital Management of Careggi, to whom it still belongs.

The twentieth-century lunette offers the villa in a new and simplified form compared to its representation in Zocchi's eighteenth-century painting; both the point it is viewed from and the layout of trees and vegetation are altered.

The left façade of the construction is shown, lightened by well-spaced windows and dominated by the bulky central section crowned with its crenellated gallery. The façade continues round the back, flaunting an elegant loggia with Ionic columns, open on three sides.

In the distance on the left of the painting (just like in Zocchi's view), a fortress can be made out - the Careggi estate farmhouse, though, nowadays, it is the convent of the Oblate Sisters of Santa Maria Nuova.

C. CONFORTI, *Le residenze di campagna dei Granduchi,* in: *Citta, ville e fortezze nella Toscana del XVIII secolo,* Florence 1978, p. 17.

Careggi
Tempera on canvas
Anonymous
Beg. XX cent.

CAREGGI

Cerreto Guidi

Literature on art has always attributed Grand Duke Francesco I de' Medici with the construction of the villa at Cerreto Guidi on account of the fact that, with the lack of reliable documentation, one could reasonably place such an enterprise at the moment when the Medicean villas were blossoming out all over the Tuscan territory.

During my research on the villa, to be published shortly, I came across documents which throw a new light on the Medici family property.

It is especially interesting to read that in 1566, among the property of Cosimo de' Medici was: "A newly-built edifice at Cerreto Guidi, placed on the Cerreto hill next to the parish church, built by His Distinguished Excellency for personal use". The specification "newly-built" gives us the first reliable date regarding the foundation of the building, which can thus be traced back to the time of Cosimo I and numbered, without a shadow of doubt, among the first Medicean exploits on Tuscan soil.

(This document confirms the hypothesis formulated by Atzori-Regoli, who reckoned the years of 1565/67 as the probable construction period because it was then that the peasants of Montopoli had apparently been called to such work). The site had probably been bought directly from the community of Cerreto, from whom, as the same document proves, Cosimo had also bought other land in that period, with contracts signed by Giovan Battista Giordani. Unfortunately no document reveals the name of the architect responsible for construction.

The work is attributed to the architect Bernardo Buontalenti on the basis of a quotation from Alfonso Parigi's work notes which reads: "1575. On last feast day which was of the Holy Ghost, I went with Master Bernardo Buontalenti to Cerreto and he passed over the work to me and I continued with 10 or 12 workmen."

In a recent analysis of Buontalenti's work, Fara makes a net distinction between the central body of the villa and the sweep of steps below: he declares that the latter were executed by Alfonso Parigi on the basis of a plan that Buontalenti probably drew up after his experiences at Pratolino and Belvedere, but he does not hazard a guess about the author of the building on account of all the work carried out on it over the years.

The architectonic complex displays some very original constructive elements which find no equivalent in other Tuscan architecture of the period. One must remember the date of construction, prior to 1566, that means before the blossoming of villas commissioned by Grand Dukes Francesco and Ferdinando.

It is very difficult to surmise who was the architect carrying out the construction work. At the relevant time Bernardo Buontalenti must have been about nineteen years old; his first recognised architectonic work is the mansion of Bianca Cappello, built in Via Maggio, Florence, in 1568. One cannot exclude that some years previously, when, already a member of the Medici court, a juvenile Buontalenti, on his return in 1562 from a journey to Spain, had had practice in architectonic composition, poring over a stock of manuals known at that time. Thus one could consider Buontalenti as the author of the building and the splendid staircase below that joins the defined volume of the construction to the asperity of the rockface underneath.

The Medicean grand dukes often stayed at the villa with their courts in any season of the year, as the place offered, besides the pleasures of the hunt, the facilities of a stop-over point on the journeys to and from Pisa.

Isabella de' Medici, daughter of Cosimo I and Eleonora of Toledo and wife of Paolo Giordano Orsini, Duke of Bracciano, met her death in the villa at Cerreto Guidi. This death, even now shrouded in mystery, has for centuries constituted the cue for the fabrication of legends and gory stories concerning the various members of the Medici family. Recent studies have cast light on the life of Isabella, discrediting the legends of iniquities, turpitudes and incest, which had originated in the eighteenth century in the atmosphere of revolt against the Medicis and which had continued into the nineteenth century, the very same episodes acquiring this time an aura of romance.

At the time of Isabella's death the villa belonged to Don Giovanni de' Medici, who had received it as a gift from Cosimo in 1567. Don Giovanni died in 1621 without legitimate heirs and his estate passed to Don Lorenzo, son of Great Duke Ferdinando I.

When Don Lorenzo died, his brother (who in the meantime had become grand duke with the name of Cosimo II) donated the villa to his own son, Cardinal Leopoldo. The first inventory of the villa at Cerreto Guidi that we know of can be traced back to that time and precisely 1667.

On the death of Cardinal Leopoldo in 1675, the property was transferred to Grand Duke Cosimo II. At a distance of just a few years (1705 and 1728) two detailed inventories of the assets kept in the villa were drawn up.

In 1739 the upkeep of the property at Cerreto was entrusted to private businesses who guaranteed, with contracts renewed every six years, all work necessary to keep the building in a good state.

The report included with the first contract described a state of serious decline of the whole complex; we can accordingly deduce that the villa had not been used as a holiday place and stop-over point for the grand duchy court for a long time.

To judge by the reports submitted by the various administrators of Crown property, the villa kept its structure and original furnishings intact until 1781, when Grand Duke Peter Leopold of Lorraine decided to get rid of the estate. The villa, together with the "hunters' lodge" (the nearby farm-house) was put up for auction: two successive auctions passed unattended; so four small-holdings removed from the farm property of Stabbia were added to the lot. The Tonini family from Pescia purchased the property, but after a few years they in turn sold it to the Maggi family from Leghorn. In 1821 the latter laid the carriage road (called "new road") that leads up to the square in front of the church and they are responsible for some internal work on the villa, such as the neoclassical decorations on the walls in some of the rooms.

In 1827 "renewal" work on the nearby parish church of San Leonardo was started: the delicate arcade that surrounded the building was substituted with a heavy loggia containing a corridor leading to the farm-house; the sides of the church were opened up to make lateral naves; furthermore the height of the main nave was raised, the choir stalls and a new vestry were built. Little remains of the antique Medicean parish church which appears in Zocchi's eighteenth-century view (and in the twentieth-century lunette that is based on it): just the lower part of the façade and the railed verandah belonging privately to the villa.

The Marquis Geddes da Filicaja of Florence bought the villa and annexes in 1885.

During the second World War, the villa was garrison headquarters and underwent sacking.

In 1966, Galliano Boldrini, a native of Cerreto Guidi, purchased the building and in 1969 donated the monumental complex to the State to have it turned into a National Museum.

The State accepted the donation with presidential decree nr. 90 of 18th November 1972.

V. Giovannozzi, *La vita di Bernardo Buontalenti scritta da Gherardo Silvani,* in: *Rivista d'Arte,* series II, Year IV, Florence 1932, p. 522.

L. Atzori, I. Regoli, *Due comuni rurali del dominio fiorentino del sec. XVI: Montopoli Val d'Arno e Castelfranco di Sotto,* in: *Archichettura e politica da Cosimo I a Ferdinando I,* ed. G. Spini, Florence 1976, p. 79.

A. Fara, *L'architettura delle ville buontalentiane nei documenti,* in: *Città, ville e fortezze nella Toscana del XVIII secolo,* Florence 1978, p. 27.

G. Micheli, *Cerreto Guidi tra cronaca e storia,* Tyrrhene/Pisa 1985.

Cerreto
Tempera on canvas
Anonymous
Beg. XX cent.

CERRETO

Poggio Imperiale

Situated on the hill just outside the Roman Gate - the ancient San Piero Gattolini Gate - the villa of Poggio Imperiale kept its original denomination of Poggio Baroncelli (after the family who were owners in the fifteenth century) right up till halfway through the seventeenth-century.

The property became a Medici possession in 1565, following the confiscation of the Salviati family assets, among which was this villa.

Cosimo I donated it to his daughter Isabella, who lived there with her husband, Paolo Giordano Orsini; on Isabella's death the property was transferred to their son, Don Virginio Orsini, and then to his son, Don Paolo Giordano Orsini II, who sold it in 1622 to Maria Magdalena of Austria, wife of Grand Duke Cosimo II.

The archduchess, of Austrian origin and specifically of the imperial family, decided to make it her own residence, considering its relative vicinity to the court which was held at the Pitti Palace at that time.

The architect Giulio Parigi completely restored and renovated the building. On termination of these works, the villa - "at this point worthy of taking on the functions of a royal palace" (Panichi) - was renamed "villa on the Imperial Hill" with an edict of 23rd May 1624. The amount of land surrounding the villa was also increased: over just a few years, five new small-holdings with relative country-houses were purchased and these went to make up the big "farm of Poggio Imperiale". The estate counted sixteen small-holdings, the land of which stretched to the San Piero Gattolini Gate, flanked on the right by part of the Sienese Road (the ancient Via Romana), and, on the other side, it extended to the top of the hill which looked over the villa, and was bordered on the left in part by the city walls and in part by the estates of rich Florentine families. The villa maintained unaltered its eighteenth-century lay-out up to the end of the century. Recalling the eighteenth-century panorama by Zocchi, the lunette shows the villa as it still appeared in the first half of 1700: the central façade is strictly traditional and compact with its line-up of windows arrayed on either side of the central group of elements the portal/terrace/balustrade reminiscent of Buontalenti. It is crowned at the top and closed in at the sides by a walled wing that, at the centre, simulates a roof-terrace and, at the sides, two one-storeyed *avant-corps* covered by terraces, which actually hide the two Italian gardens on either side of the villa.

The semi-circular, statue-adorned balustrade finishes off the façade and circumscribes the lawn in front of the villa.

At the time of Grand Duke Peter Leopold of Lorraine (1765/1790), the Poggio Imperiale property still constituted one of the most important Crown possessions. The grand duke had the villa completely renovated following the plans of the architect Gaspare Maria Paoletti. The works of transformation took place from 1766 to 1783. The interior was entirely restructured and decorated with stuccoes, following the latest neo-classical trend; the two side gardens were turned into courtyards with the wings of the building enclosing them; the rear façade was re-planned; the principal one, however, remained unchanged. The architect Giuseppe Cacialli completely redid the latter in 1807, expanding the plans of the architect Pasquale Poccianti, pupil of Paoletti.

These final works gave the building the aspect that it still presents today.

At the time when Florence was capital of Italy (1865), the villa became the Santissima Annunziata Boarding School for Girls, a function which it still keeps today.

C. DA PRATO, *Villa del Poggio Imperiale oggi Istituto della SS. Annunziata, storia e descrizione,* Florence 1895.

M. MARANGONI, *La villa del Poggio Imperiale,* Florence 1923.

N. BEMPORAD, D. MIGNANI, O. PANICHI, *Villa del Poggio Imperiale. Lavori di restauro e di riordinamento 1972-75,* Florence 1975.

D. MIGNANI, *Un'idea di giardino moderno per un giardino prospettico. Il progetto di trosformozione del giardino della villa medicea del Poggio Imperiale,* in: *Il giardino romantico,* Florence 1986, p. 46.

Poggio Imperiale
Tempera on canvas
Anonymous
Beg. XX cent.

POGGIO IMPERIALE

Printed by *Gramma* - Perugia
March 2004